The New Romantics

Adrian Berg, *Gloucester Lodge, Regent's Park*, 1980, acrylic

Original colour graphic by
ADRIAN BERG

Derwent Fells with Skiddaw from the Foot of Latrigg is a panoramic view of the Lake District landscape created this autumn by the artist specially for *Art & Design*. Each strip can be combined to form a single panorama that runs from left to right. The end of the final strip can be united with the beginning of the first to form the full panorama.

Andy Goldsworthy, *Line to explore colours in leaves, calm, overcast*
Ouchiyama-mura, Japan, 14 November 1987

An Art & Design Profile

The New Romantics

Anselm Kiefer, *Saturn Time*, 1986

ACADEMY EDITIONS · LONDON / ST MARTIN'S PRESS · NEW YORK

Acknowledgements

Front cover (detail) and title page: Anselm Kiefer, *Saturn Time*, 1986, oil, acrylic, emulsion, shellac, crayon and photographs on canvas, with ferns and lead (From the Anselm Kiefer retrospective organised by James Speyer of the Art Institute of Chicago and Mark Rosenthal of the Philadelphia Museum of Art, a touring exhibition currently at MOMA, New York); *Back cover:* Sandro Chia, *Decoration*, 1988, encaustic and oil; *Inside front cover:* Christopher Le Brun, *Tower and Tree*, 1987, oil (Nigel Greenwood Gallery); *Inside back cover:* Mimmo Paladino, *South*, 1984, bronze; *half-title:* Adrian Berg, *Gloucester Lodge, Regent's Park*, 1980, acrylic (Courtesy the artist, photo Prudence Cumming Associates); *frontispiece:* Andy Goldsworthy, *Line to explore colours in leaves, calm, overcast*, Ouchiyama-mura, Japan, 14 November 1987 (from *Andy Goldsworthy: Mountain and Coast – Autumn into Winter Japan 1987*, Yurakucho-Asahi); *Contents page:* Francesco Clemente, *Untitled*, 1985, oil (Anthony d'Offay Gallery)

We should like to thank the following galleries who provided illustrations of works illustrated in this issue:

Romanticism and Retrospection
pp6-19: the Saatchi Collection for Kiefer, Anthony d'Offay for Clemente and Cucchi, Fabian Carlsson for Goldsworthy, the Piccadilly Gallery for Arnold and Ovenden, the Dokumenta 8 exhibition for Laib, Nicola Jacobs for Mach, the Museum of Contemporary Art, Los Angeles, for Turrell, and the exhibition *Individuals: A Selected History of Contemporary Art 1945-86* for Heizer.

Romanticism: A Definition
pp20-27: the Fitzwilliam Museum for the Palmer, the National Gallery, London, for Delacroix (p21), the Tate Gallery for Blake and Fuseli, the Fogg Art Gallery for Delacroix (p23), the National Gallery, Scotland, for Constable, and the Musée des Beaux-Arts, Lyon, for Géricault.

Concepts of Romanticism
pp28-35: Marlborough Fine Art for Oulton, the *Hang zur Architektur* exhibition at the German Architecture Museum, Frankfurt, for Hödicke and Lüpertz, the Nigel Greenwood Gallery for Wiszniewski, Anthony d'Offay for Beuys, the Raab Gallery for Currie, Marlborough Fine Art for Oulton, and the Tate Gallery for Blake.

English Neo-Romantics
pp36-41: the Arts Council of Great Britain for Piper, Ayrton and Minton, the British Council for Sutherland, the Tate Gallery for Craxton, and Gillian Jason for Vaughan.

Romanticism and the Modernist Myth
pp42-9: the Tate Gallery for Turner, Constable and Braque, Marlborough Fine Art for Oulton, Nigel Greenwood for Le Brun, the Galeria Joan Pratz for Amat.

Ruralism and the New Romanticism
pp50-52: the Piccadilly Gallery for Arnold.

New Romantic Artists
pp53-60: the Tate Gallery for Moore and Chia, Glasgow Art Gallery for Colquhoun, Galerie Michael Werner for Immendorff, Anthony d'Offay for Beuys and Long, Solomon R Guggenheim Museum for Cucchi, Nigel Greenwood for Le Brun and Wiszniewski, Marlborough Fine Art for Oulton.

Romantically Inclined
pp61-7: the Tate Gallery for Turner and Lanyon, Towner Art Gallery, Eastbourne for Ravilious.

Modern Myths
pp68-73: this article draws its theme, and some of its illustrations, from the exhibition *Classical Myths* organised by the Boise Gallery, Idaho. The McKenna came from Edward Totah, the Albert from the Raab Gallery and the Garouste from *Falls the Shadow*, Hayward Gallery, 1986. David Ligare supplied transparencies of his own works.

Romantic Sculpture
pp 74-80: Michael Werner in Cologne for Lüpertz, Waddington for Paladino, Lisson Gallery for Deacon, Karsten Schubert for Wilding and Houshiary, and the Hayward Gallery exhibition *Falls the Shadow* for Laib. Stephen Cox provided the illustration of his own work.

Editor: Dr Andreas C Papadakis

First published in Great Britain in 1988 by Art & Design
an imprint of the
ACADEMY GROUP LTD, 7 HOLLAND STREET, LONDON W8 4NA

ISBN 0-85670-956-5 (UK)

Art & Design Profile 12 is published as part of Art & Design Volume 4 11/12-1988
Distributed in the United States of America by
ST MARTIN'S PRESS, 175 FIFTH AVENUE, NEW YORK 10010
ISBN 0-312-03065-7 (US)

Printed in Singapore

Contents

Francesco Clemente, *Untitled*, 1985, oil

Anselm Kiefer, *Father, Son, Holy Ghost*, 1973, oil and charcoal on burlap

ROMANTICISM AND RETROSPECTION
An Interview with Robert Rosenblum

Enzo Cucchi, *Untitled*, 1984, watercolour

Contemporary art is characterised by a fascination with the history of art. The spirit of retrospection can be seen as the manifestation of a revival of interest in Romanticism. Here Robert Rosenblum, author of the influential *Modern Painting and the Northern Romantic Tradition: Friedrich to Rothko*, discusses with Hugh Cumming the role of Romanticism in current art, its various manifestations and its relationship to new international movements.

– *Do you think that the tradition you discerned in your book* The Northern Romantic Tradition *is important to painting at the moment in any way?*
There is no more impossible word than Romanticism and though I use it, as does everybody else, very casually and carelessly, I would be very hard put to define it. It is of course infinitely contractable and expandable. In terms of the general patterns that I try to trace in that book, were I to write a supplementary chapter to it – I stopped with Rothko and Abstract Expressionism – I would probably include earthworks of the late 60s and 70s. Those seem in some way to be the last gasp of that tradition of trying to find some sort of connection with the Great Beyond or the Void. My own sense of what might be called Romantic today, in so far as it resembles in an obvious way historical Romanticism, is really part of the whole constellation of 'neo' movements so that what one thinks of as Neo-Classicism, whether by Finlay or Mariani, is to be thought of in the same category as works by Christopher Le Brun which look to me like neo-Gustave Moreau or neo-symbolist painting. The Romanticism of the present is really Romanticism in terms of historical retrospection and reflects the whole condition of neo-ism, revivalism and retrospection that we have in the 1980s as opposed to being an organic continuation of earlier traditions. The big historical break in continuity took place in the 1960s and 70s and anything younger today is likely to be wilfully self-consciously retrospective rather than part of the same tradition.
– *So you see contemporary Romanticism as essentially a form of nostalgia?*

It's just part of the whole tradition of the revival of earlier styles from the 19th and 20th century. The revival say of Gothic architecture in the 1980s or even Gothic furniture could nominally be categorised as Romantic in so far as the Middle Ages is regarded as a token of Romantic revival, but it really is better seen in the same spirit as the revival of Mondrian or even Barnett Newman. It's just a question of the incredible environment we have of history and art history and just one facet of reconstructing it in the 1980s.
– *So would you see Phillip Taaffe for example as a Romantic?*
In so far as one thinks of revivalism or historicism as Romantic, then he is. The better way to put it is that any neo-Romantic artist of the 1980s is like Phillip Taaffe, that artist however is reviewing or resurrecting a different mode of history.
– *Some people have a very fixed idea of what Romanticism is. If you think of the number of landscapes of whatever type, skill or inclination that are painted, people will always buy or appreciate that kind of art and that is their view of Romanticism. Do you think that is something that exists outside the mainstream of art?*
I assume that there are always artists of a provincial or insular kind who are remote from the more sophisticated centres who will go on for example doing watercolours of landscapes and inject into them some kind of traditional sentimentality and I guess these can be considered vestigial Romantics' explorations of a long and great tradition. There are, on the same wave length, in the States for example, younger painters who are not continuing so much as reviving Romantic landscape, such as Diane Burko and April Gornik who not so much resurrect landscape

Richard Long, *Mountain Lake Powder Snow*, 1985, Lapland

traditions of sublime mountain heights à la Friedrich or Hödler, or even the tradition of painting vast gloomy expanses, foggy skies and infinite horizons in the northern Romantic landscape tradition. But they do it again quite self-consciously as a revival style just in the way that Mariani or Finlay would revive the look of Neo-Classicism of the late 18th and early 19th century. I think that is really the deeper affinity between their works. The Romantic and Classical artists that we have now are really all manifestations of the same retrospection. It's just the way that Phillip Johnson can do a building in a Gothic mode as well as in a Classical mode now. That very eclecticism is again part too of the historicism of the early 19th century. So its a kind of double revival, it's a Chinese Box situation, of now a revival of styles being a revival of that kind of eclecticism that characterised so much Romantic painting and architecture.

– *Do you think that Romanticism exists as a style rather than there being another aspect to it, for instance, nature as a source of the spiritual and sublime?*

I think what's Romantic in the grandest sense is the retrospection. It seems to me that all these artists of the 1980s are in a way fleeing the present by living in history, but this has been done so many times before and we are living in far more desperate and ironic age that it has to be done with lighter touch. Nobody believes that these are going to be therapeutic changes and therefore it's all done as it were in quotation marks.

– *Is there a social or spiritual ideal or some system of belief or way of life that people look to, or is it just a visual world?*

I honestly think that most high-minded ideals about art and morality, art and society, art and Utopia have been almost completely dashed. A stake has been driven through the heart of all optimistic beliefs in art as a goal for purification and change. That's certainly my impression from the younger generations in New York. There may be some last-gasp geniuses like James Turrell for example who still is, like Caspar David Friedrich's monk by the sea, all alone looking at the universe and the night sky, and he's great. But in general a younger 1980s generation is living very much here and now in the world of art as commerce, communication and computer systems. I think there are precious few artists of any real interest today who claim for art some kind of spiritual and moral force in the modern world.

The whole Romantic tradition of ruins, having melancholy thoughts about ruins, has had new lease of life in the 1970s and

Andy Goldsworthy, *Japanese maple leaves stitched together to make a floating chain,* 21 Nov 1987, Ouchiyama-mura, Japan

Anselm Kiefer, *Flight of the Ladybird*, 1974, oil on burlap

80s with people like the Poiriers or, even in the States, Charles Simmonds-sort of archaeological fantasies. But they again don't have the grand historical wallop that they had when they were originally invented and experienced at the end of the 18th century when they had to do with the great cycles of civilisation. I mean it really is done more as a kind of quotation or with a kind of chic irony about an earlier way of feeling and seeing. So no matter what you do it seems to be separated by a vast historical gulf. It's art as an imitation of past historical revisions, past imagery, past emotions; it never seems first- hand.

— *Is that what essentially distinguishes the attitude towards the past? Do you think there's a reverence towards the past or a respect for the past or a kind of anaesthetised feeling towards it, that there's such a great separation that it doesn't have any bearing any more?*

It's just become common coinage. There's been such an enormous dissemination of art history today and everything has become interchangeable. David Salle for example can just throw in quotes from Watteau, Géricault, Reginald Marsh, Kunisoshi or Riopelle, it doesn't seem to make any difference. It's just a question of juggling images and devaluing them all. I don't in

any way mean to suggest that therefore artists who do this are less good than artists who don't, but that this is the condition we all live in, as you can tell by looking at the museum shop anywhere in the world.

An artist I would think of as still perpetuating an older unbroken tradition of Romanticism is Richard Long who really doesn't have the irony of the 1980s, but he's been doing this for a long time. If I had to have a candidate for somebody who perpetuated the imagery, the feelings, the emotions of someone like Constable or Wordsworth, I'd vote for him.

— *What is it about his work that is associated with the best of traditional Romanticism? Some people would see him as separate from it.*

He is somebody who really continues those endless magical communions with nature by talking, touching, feeling and accumulating. I find this very direct in terms of his experience and really very moving as a kind of endangered species, but it still works with him. I think he is the last of his race.

— *There's another artist called Andy Goldsworthy – who is slightly similar to Richard Long. He seems to have a greater sense of pattern and colour. He collects berries and leaves and*

Anselm Kiefer, *Wayland's Song (with Wing)*, 1982, oil, emulsion, straw on photo, on canvas with lead

combines them often in a more imaginative way .
There's a German artist Wolfgang Laib who does something of this sort too. He spends a lot of time in the woods gathering such things as pollen and collecting it and forming minimal geometric patterns out of gossamer and natural materials such as honey or dust of various kinds. It is some kind of ecological last gasp of communion with some pure beautiful stuff of nature. I guess this attitude is expiring even though it may, as in the case of Richard Long, still produce some marvellous artists.
– *Do think there is an equivalent in painting? Are there any artists who are not so much copying or reviving previous styles but drawing on them in a new way? Do you think landscape or nature is a source for imagery distinct from that of the past?*
In the examples that I suggested earlier, Diane Burko and April Gornak, they are in fact in the tradition of sublime landscape painting, but they still seem to produce it in terms of an ironic knowing way as if they were not continuing this tradition in an intuitive ongoing manner but somehow wilfully resurrecting it in the way say Philip Johnson might resurrect a Gothic cathedral.

I think that Kiefer might certainly have some claim to being a living survivor of the endangered species of German Romantic painting. He sometimes seems to echo in the direction of Friedrich. But then I also feel too that this is a kind of Post-Modern situation and he's so filled with historical retrospection not only in terms of German history but German painting especially, Friedrich or German Neo-Classical architecture. He also belongs to the category of historical quotation from the other side of the gulf. I have to confess that I have been susceptible to his epic sweep. There is a feel in Kiefer that, for want of a better word, I would call Romantic, somebody who has the grandeur of Victor Hugo, somebody who has a giant retrospection looking back over a nation's past, immediate and remote. This is done in a very heartfelt thrilling way. I would think seriously about Kiefer as a candidate for continuing – I'm not quite sure whether it's the real thing or a post-neo-thing a grand panoramic tradition of German culture and art.

The word Romanticism is so slippery in semantic terms that the meaning of it could be stretched to include a wide range of artistic activity these days which involves a sort of personal introspection rather than historical retrospection. This has usually again been thought of as one of the products of the Romantic movement, the ability of artists to present psycho-biography in their work.

Artists like this, Jasper Johns especially in recent years, paint pictures that are practically intimate journal entries. This is relatively new I think in terms of 20th-century art and it may be some curious permutation of a Romantic progeny. Many of the works of Clemente in terms of their exploration of his own sexuality, fantasies, dreams and nightmares belong in that way to this tradition and probably not so much in a self-conscious historical quoting way but in terms of an ordinary human need to explore private feelings. One could think about that as a more recent manifestation of Romantic attitudes. But those may just be human constants, the need for personal revelation.

The Johns' paintings, the quartet of the cycle of the four seasons are just heart-breakingly intimate tragic comments on the passing of time, nature, personal biography and so on. As such they really seem to extend the great traditions of the history of Western art, in particular of Romantic identity with nature. But he's an artist of an earlier generation and probably can still work within that mode. He was doing that kind of personal projection diary-entry art already at the beginning of the 1950s. It's just a more complicated version now.
– *What do you find particularly tragic?*

He's imposed the pattern of the four seasons upon himself and adapted his personal intimate biography as well as his professional artistic public biography upon that scheme.
– *Do you feel that there's anyone else dealing with those kind of themes at the moment?*
Not on that level. As I mentioned, artists like Clemente certainly explore issues, like love and death in personal terms but they do it in a far more lightweight, capricious way than Johns. He is a master and the recent work is in some ways a summation of three decades of his art, so it has an experience and mastery of all kinds of energies behind it. On the other hand it's interesting to compare it to the kind of retrospection and work of another artist of Johns' generation, Roy Lichtenstein, who in the 1980s has also done any number of inventories of his past achievements. But he's always doing it in a kind of tongue-in-cheek way. Although one might think about these as a kind of personal and public retrospection it has – and that's the whole point of Lichtenstein – none of the potent emotions that are so apparent in Johns' work.
– *One of the things that characterises traditional Romanticism especially in poetry, is the incredible sense of awe and excite-*

L to R: Wolfgang Laib, *Hazelnut Pollen*, Dokumenta 8; James Turrell, *Skyspace I*, 1972, interior light with open sky

They seem to be personal projections of his own life viewed against the passing seasons. That's a traditional theme, God knows, in Western art. The pictures not only have that universal aspect of going from spring to winter but also all kinds of cryptic as well as decypherable references to his own art, biography, and past. They're very meditative, they're like the works of some late great poet who is contemplating his life, his career, his future against the aspect of eternity. They really are very directly moving in the grand old tradition rather than being infused with a kind of detachment or cynicism that seems to characterise most younger artists who have emerged in the last ten years or so.
– *It's interesting that in those paintings he uses a lot of imagery and obviously structures the paintings with a traditional theme when he has been celebrated for his desire not to use imagery. Do you think that is part of the spirit of times, this move towards using imagery and a structural device like the seasons?*
I think he's always liked some kind of system to cling to, some sort of impersonal pattern, whether it be alphabets, or numbers or the structure of the American flag, the Stars and Stripes, or the map of the States. In this particular case he likes the imposed order – it's like a poet deciding to use sonnet form or sestina.

ment and sentimental ecstasy and liberation that is represented by landscape. In a different way someone like Blake, both in his paintings and his poetry, has a spiritual visionary side to his imagination that gave him a kind of aesthetic and social conviction that there is a particular way of seeing things that is uplifting and that is contrary to the way life is led. Do you think that that particular attitude is something that people don't hold or can't have in art at the moment?
It seems very ingenuous to me these days. I have the feeling that the last really important artists who felt things like that were the Abstract Expressionists, and then extending that, I would think that some of the people like Robert Smithson or Michael Heizer or Walter de Maria, and above all James Turrell who I admire endlessly, belong to this category of lonely visionaries. But in the big cities where most of the art is made and seen and sold it's a pretty rare attitude. William Blake was doing it in London. I don't know if anybody's doing it in London today, but certainly not in New York.
– *I suppose the sinister side of Romanticism that appreciates fear and terror and the more devious side of human nature, that comes with fantasy, would appeal more to the modern spirit.*

In a way Andy Warhol summed it up when he reported on the earthquake in the south of Italy, near Naples, that killed presumably about 10,000 people. A great Romantic painter would have perhaps painted a huge disaster picture with memories of the eruption of Vesuvius in 79 AD, Andy Warhol just replicated the front page of the Italian newspaper that reported on it. I can't think of a better way to extinguish that Romantic catastrophe tradition. So Andy Warhol as usual marks a profound change between BC and AD in the history of later 20th-century art.
– *What characterises his attitude?*
He won't take it personally, he sees it always in terms of the mass distribution of what used to be a private response. He was the first artist of major significance to sense the realities of reproduction, of commercialisation of art, of commodity, of distribution of information in the 1960s and 70s. He's really the one who killed this definitively. That's an amazing achievement. I think he pinpointed the total change in our times.
- *So you think that is a characteristic aesthetic attitude of our times, not to become emotionally involved?*
It's rather like what Manet did when he painted the execution of Maximilian or when he painted the escape of Henri Rochefort

otherwise we'd have a very strange selection. So the bottom line is still in the way it looks.
– *Would it have to be some stylistic legacy aside from a concern with nature that someone would draw on today?*
Yes, it would really be the most superficial aspect of Romanticism, namely a kind of copying, a kind of eclectic mimicking of the look of the subject matter of the as it were authentic Romantics who were concerned, with, for instance, ruins, or some kind of melancholic revival of antiquity, or some fascination with disaster, danger, the irrational. To do that today means in effect producing a TV programme on it in the form of works of art. It's just reportorial or encyclopaedic, but I don't think it's going to be felt in the same manner.
– *The main attempt to establish a contemporary Romantic school in Britain was the Brotherhood of Ruralists with Peter Blake, David Inshaw, Graham Arnold and Graham Ovenden. For a time they tried to establish a Romantic landscape school that drew on certain myths and literary images to create an idealised personal idyll.*
I guess that in itself is a symptom of historicising nostalgia. British artists were doing that in the 30s and 40s, trying to revive

Michael Heizer, *Double Negative*, 1969-70, 240,000 ton displacement in rhyolite and sandstone, Mormon Mesa, Nevada

from a Penal Colony in the South Seas: there's just no overt drama the way Géricault or Goya would have done it. It's just a kind of newsflash. That was one way of killing Romantic vestiges in terms of the modern urban situation in Paris. In the 60s and 70s I think Warhol did the same thing, and did it pretty definitively now.
– *Is that something that you admire, is that a viewpoint you hold yourself?*
It's not a question of admiring, it's a question of being a spectator. I think that, one, yes, that's true, that's the way things are more and more, and that's the way they've certainly become in the last 30 years; and, two, I happen to think that Warhol is a great artist for, among other reasons, the fact he took on this cultural phenomenon and turned it into art. He reflects it. If I think that the human situation involved is lamentable, it is nevertheless a fact, and I can't blame Warhol for bringing the news to everybody, he is just reflecting it. So it's not about good or bad. Anyway I'm enough of an old-fashioned aesthete in personal terms to think that we're after all talking about art and not culture. Art has it's own hierarchy of good and bad and we don't judge works of art on the basis of what the human messages are,

Samuel Palmer and his world. I guess there will always be that cycle.
– *Some people claim that Britain is the home of a sort of intrinsic Romantic tradition associated with landscape and nature. Is that valid?*
It may well be because one of the things that is always fascinating about Britain to an outsider is that it does seem more insular (literally and figuratively) than other countries, and doesn't seem usually to be clocked by the same time machines as the rest of the Western world. It may well be that if there are pockets of continuing Romanticism in the West, Britain's probably the best place to find them. I guess there's been more of a geographical and cultural shedding-off of the rest of the 20th century in Britain than there has been in most other industrialised developed countries.
– *Is it a sort of anachronism?*
It's just out of sync. If you're clocking it by the international Western time I guess it is anachronistic, like the monarchy and attitudes towards the House of Windsor. But if you live here and that's the major way of telling time and seeing things, then the rest of the world may seem out of joint.

Enzo Cucchi, *A Painting That Barely Touches the Sea*, 1983, oil and wood on canvas

- *Another aspect of the interest in Romanticism is the revival of interest in Neo-Romanticism in Britain. Ten years ago it was ignored except by a few people. A few of the major painters who painted throughout that period were obviously recognised, but people like Minton, Ayrton, Cecil Collins and Craxton weren't so generally publicised. Now there seems to be, especially amongst the art press, a revival of interest in that era. Do you think that's anything more than an academic or historical interest?*

Perhaps in terms of the dynamics of British art and culture there's some significant trend here, but, looking at it more internationally, there has been such an incredible archaeological unearthing of various suppressed moments of 20th-, not to mention 19th-century art, that it may be nothing more than a symptom of this voracious desire to uncover all of our historical past. In the United States for example there have been all kinds of younger art historians working on American artists of the 1940s in particular, who were passed by because of the stampede of Abstract Expressionism. But the same is true of the 1930s and 20s, you name it. It's just this ongoing encyclopaedic eagerness to uncover it all. So my more cynical view would be to suggest that very often these revivals of the past are not so much a response to a particular fascination or affinity with the art but simply a part of the ongoing obsessive historicism to disclose more and more of what the Modern Movement had hidden, and the same thing is happening with the 19th century galore.

- *So people aren't looking at those works because they particularly like Romantic art of that description?*

One likes it, but one always should remember that history is aesthetics as well, that is one very often enjoys looking at works of art because they emanate nostalgia for a particular period. When we look at Art Deco, for example, part of the reason that we enjoy looking at it is that we like the feel of the 1920s and 30s, just as the 1950s and 60s have terrific charges, so that any work of art that has a period flavour seems to be a time capsule of magic moments in the past. There's a whole concept of history as aesthetics, of works of art that radiate the flavour of a particular decade, period and so on, and produce that association in themselves. The interest in Neo-Romanticism in Britain at least may in good part be a kind of nostalgia for the 30s and 40s. But one feels nostalgia for everything in the 20th century it seems to me. I can't wait for the 70s revival; the 60s are there already.

Christopher Le Brun, *Grove*, 1987, oil

— *So you don't feel that an obsessive nostalgia for the past and previous styles and forms is necessarily a bad thing?*
I don't think it's bad or good. Jacques Louis David was a great artist and he made great works out of an excessive fascination with history and the art of the past, and so did Picasso, other artists will just fall on their faces doing the same thing. I just think it's a question of individual genius or lack of it.
— *Are there any younger artists particularly in Britain that you would see as drawing on Romanticism in any way?*
In a strange way I find David Mach rather fascinating as an artist who will upset conventions. He's a model, a demonstration of Romantic chaos. One of the things that's so thrilling about his work is that he just breaks all barriers literally and figuratively and things just come bursting through the walls and the windows. It's like the equivalent of being confronted, if you were a Romantic voyager or painter, with Niagara Falls. A lot of the images do have the overtone of the end of the world, some sort of debris that is left after the apocalypse. On the other hand, very characteristic of the 80s, it's success depends upon the fact that it's done with a certain amount of detachment and irony. I love *The Hundred and One Dalmations*. It's just that introduction of a

Walt Disney myth into what could also look like the aftermath of bombing, and the confusion of those two things give it a very contemporary flavour, so that you weren't allowed to take it as seriously which would have been the case had it been a Romantic artist painting the aftermath of the destruction of Pompeii and Herculaeneum. So he is somebody who might be thought of in the kind of crazy category of Romantic disaster images that have been tailored to 1980s cynicism.
— *What do you think someone like Adrian Wiszniewski who does very Romantic portraits and scenes of Byronic figures against a very ornate kind of William Morris background?*
It's true. Or even Steven Campbell too. Those artists look to me very eclectic, as though they are reviving wilfully, the way Christopher Le Brun does, the look of a lot of early Romantic painting. I don't mean that as bad. An Italian painter like Enzo Cucchi very often paints these pictures of Romantic desolation. They look like after the bomb. They do however have a sense of paraphrase of earlier apocalyptic images. Robert Morris does the same thing. He has painted so many end-of-the-world pictures. But they're also very chic and stylish and that sort of saves them from bathos because it's an impossible subject.

Francesco Clemente, *Rocks and Sea,* 1985, oil

— *Do you think that Romanticism is a defunct term as its traditionally understood?*
I really think it's an impossible term to use. It's hard enough to use at the time that it's historically relevant, the later 18th and early 19th century. I talk about it all the time and realise I don't know what I mean, except that I feel I know what I mean, but couldn't articulate it. But if you expand it into the present you're on even thinner ice, as I guess the fact that we've been talking about every artist from the last 20 years indicates.
— *Do you think any of the traditional American myths about the landscape – the country as an ideal – as in the work of Andrew Wyeth, are alive today?*
I think it's only there in terms of grassroots popular imagery or fantasy. Andrew Wyeth is an artist who probably could be thought of as extending all kinds of Romantic, especially American Romantic premises. But the fact of the matter is that he seems, to sophisticated eyes at least, to be more of a commercial product, in the old-fashioned sense – not a commercial product like Haim Steinbach and Jeff Koons – than a high serious artist. Which isn't good or bad, but it's just that he's selling old-fashioned Romantic American myths the way say a movie maker

might. They have a kind of soap-opera mentality and predictable formulas and they work for vast audiences. They seem to preach loneliness, closeness to nature, hard work, the prairie, the wilderness and so on. Those are ancient Romantic myths that still have popular currency, but they certainly don't seem to have much genuine currency in the work of younger inventive artists.
— *What do you think the attitude of the younger inventive artists in America towards Romanticism would be?*
Most of them would have shut the door on it and thrown away the keys. They're interested in the realities of art and life now and especially the idea of art as commodity which sends chills up so many spines because it seems like a blasphemy in terms of early pieties about art. I think that's a very sensible motif because that is the way things are now. It's nice that some artists can be realistic enough to try to translate these underlying attitudes of our business culture now into visible works of art. I admire that kind of directness of approach, of telling things the way they are. That's one of the reasons that Warhol was so good. It doesn't necessarily make good art, but if you have an important theme like that you must be on to something.
— *So you think that commodity is a dominant interest?*

16

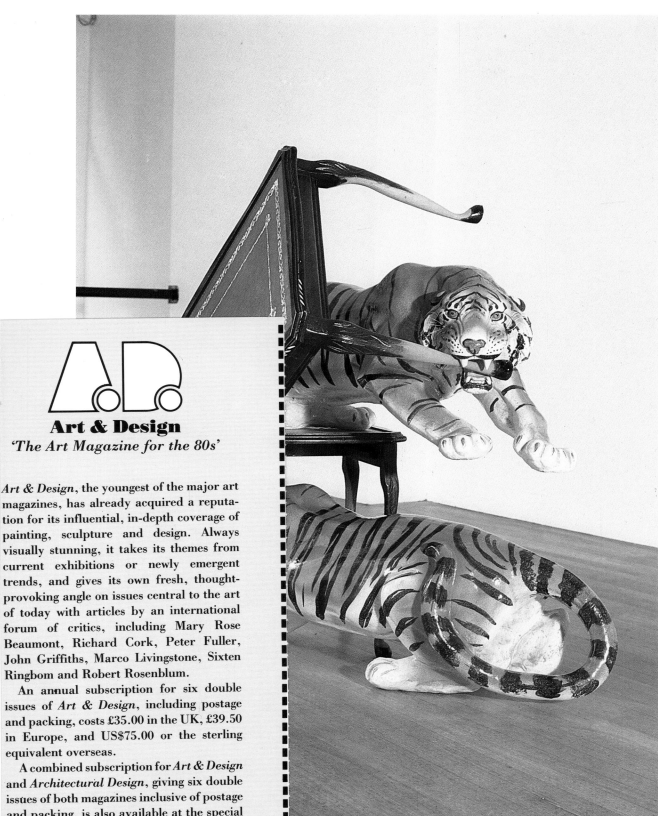

...ach, *Table for Two*, 1987, wood and ceramic

Graham Arnold, *A Quiet Gathering*, oil, 1983

I think so – I'm thinking about New York – in terms of the younger American art that makes me sit up and take notice: people like Jeff Koons or Haim Steinbach or Ashley Bickerton. I think they're fascinating, they raise all kinds of new disturbing questions. A lot of the art looks like neo-Pop art from the 60s which is the tradition of the 80s.

– *So do you think that they're saying that art is essentially a commodity to be bought and sold and it has no aesthetic value?*
No, that's the *leitmotif* of the issues that they're dealing with, of mass production, cheap multiple objects, but of course they're turning it into something that has its own aesthetic flavour. They're all working within this range of belt-line personal looking computer art of the 1980s world and putting their own stamp on it in a very conventional way, like the way in the early 1960s people would be saying that all artists of the time such as Andy Warhol and Roy Lichtenstein did was copy a comic strip or an ad in the newspaper. In fact we all know now that they were two completely different artists dealing with some of the cultural issues of the period and the counter-Romantic attitudes of the period then, but they have their own personal flavour.

– *Do you feel that the issues that Jeff Koons and Haim*

Steinbach deal with are the issues of the period?
They are very involved with the look and feel of the 1980s. But what has also become fascinating in retrospect is that they in turn have this quality of historical retrospection because they really look very like neo-60s artists. When I looked at Haim Steinbach's rows of boxes of corn flakes for example or non-edibles like bowls which you can buy in Conrans I realised this is what Andy Warhol was doing with Brillo boxes in the 60s but it has a new flavour.

– *What makes it different?*
He has his own visual rhythms which are different from Warhol's. They also look like Don Judd in terms of wall shelves and repeat modular patterns. But the fact is that he's ordered these components in a completely personal way whereas the components in the case of Warhol are completely impersonal. I find this is a group of artists who have terrific flavour and freshness and relevance, to use that revival word of the 60s. They also have that extra historical shadow of reviving the 60s. It couldn't be less Romantic.

– *Do you think that they represent the dominant tendency in American art at the moment?*

18

Graham Ovenden, *Rock Formation*, oil

One of the things that's so fascinating about art of the moment is that there isn't any dominant tendency. But certainly they are artists that command a lot of my attention. I'm very interested in art that is a reproduction of other art and that whole question of how an artist can project his whole individual personality while replicating existing works of art. But it is also a more general reflection of the whole issue of living in a world with endless reproductions.

— *Do you feel that essentially things have changed to such an extent that if you use more traditional terms such as Romanticism and Classicism it's not really not an effective way of describing what's going on?*

I really don't think so, I think that's a cop out, and I don't think they're really adequate. I don't have any new words to substitute. I think Romanticism or Neo-Classicism are alive and well today only in so far as they are part of the wide vocabulary of historical styles that have been replicated with variations by younger artists, but I don't think they are living extensions of the original movements any more than the Houses of Parliament are living extensions of Gothic secular architecture.

— *Do you think that the sense of the sublime that Rothko and*

Barnett Newman celebrated is no longer something that inspires people?

I really think that those days are over. I don't think that's for better or for worse, it's just an historical fact, like the way that people thought that art could change people's politics. I don't think there are very many people who believe it any more. A very interesting example is Leon Golub. I remember when he first showed these pictures of political prisoners tortured, mercenary soldiers, atrocities of all kinds, they were unbelievably shocking. They were intended to have not only reportorial truth but also to prick people's consciences into being aware that there were facts of the world we live in transcending the frame of the work of art. But the awful truth is, even with those most noble goals of being a journalist reporter to expose terrible unbearable truths about the world we live in, the pictures very rapidly dwindle back to an aesthetic frame and they now just look like paintings by Leon Golub and don't have the political force they were intended to have. So I think the possibility of art as a vehicle for any kind of change, moral, social or spiritual is something of the past. We're living in a much more, for better or for worse, cynical realistic time.

Samuel Palmer, *The Magic Apple Tree*, watercolour

ROMANTICISM: A DEFINITION
Michael Greenhalgh

Eugène Delacroix, *Ovid Among the Scythians*, oil

Whether one views Romanticism as an eternal state of mind or as a specific historical movement, Romanticism is not easily definable. In this article Michael Greenhalgh attempts to define the characteristics –from individuality and imagination to emotion, exoticism, mysticism, subversion – of a movement that although intricately related to a critique of the changing world of the early 19th century, offered ways forward for art in the future.

The Origins of Romanticism

Although the word itself is much older,[1] the beginnings of the Romantic movement – pre-Romanticism[2] – appear after the middle of the 18th century in Germany, England and France,[3] although which country has the primacy is a contentious matter.[4] Each country's contributions cross-fertilise the others, in all the arts,[5] but especially literature for all the important texts in French, German and English (and sometimes Italian) are immediately translated into the other languages. German works were most popular of all, especially those of A W Schlegel.[6]

Romanticism is, first and foremost, a literary movement, based on works such as Rousseau's *Julie ou la nouvelle Héloise* (1761) and *Rêveries d'un promeneur solitaire* (1782), Bernardin de Saint-Pierre's *Paul et Virginie* (1787), Thomas Gray's poems (collected 1768), James MacPherson's invention of Ossian (1760), Wackenroder & Tieck's *Herzenergiessungen eines kunstliebenden Klosterbruders* (1797), and Novalis' *Hymnen an die Nacht* (1797). As such, it generated plentiful theoretical writings, often in the guise of commentaries, such as Madame de Stael's *De l'Allemagne* or the *Vorlesungen uber dramatische Kunst und Literatur* (1809-11) of A W Schlegel, the translator of Shakespeare and Calderon. These writers, by their poetry and prose, and the critics, by their theories, proclaimed the independence of art from the restricting rules of Classicism and the primacy of the imagination and sentiment over reason. Kant was to teach that Man and Nature were not isolated the one from the other, so that nature and landscape came into their own as evocative elements which could deeply affect the human psyche,

whereas previously they had been either feared and shunned, or organised and hence tamed into formal gardens.

Indeed, in the theory of Romanticism, change in artistic *mores* was seen as inevitable: Madame de Stael, in her *De la littérature considérée dans ses rapports avec les institutions sociales* (1800), explained that the spirit of any people changed as law, institutions, religion and society changed. Hence the sources of Romanticism are to be found deep in the great changes beginning around the middle of the 18th century – from a rural to an urban population; from agriculture to industry; from a hierarchy of millenial status to the tyranny of money; from a belief in progress to a cynicism and an *ennui*[7] which could at times approach nihilism or even satanism. But whether Romanticism is a result of such changes, or only a symptom; whether it is primarily a change in mentality rather than in living conditions m such questions are unanswerable. Certainly, external changes seem to have affected the artist (in whatever medium) very deeply, so as to 'undermine permanently the range of political, social and imaginative contents available . . . a whole range of conventional, traditionally compulsive contents became useless to the artist.'[8]

Classicism and Romanticism

'Romanticism is not exactly in the choice of subject-matter or of exact truth, but in the way of feeling . . . For me Romanticism is the most recent and up-to-date expression of beauty . . . Who says *Romanticism* says *Modern art* – and that is to say intimacy, spirituality, colour, and yearning for the infinite . . . Romanticism is the child of the North, and the North is a colourist; dreams and fairy-stories are children of the mist.' (Baudelaire, in his account of the Salon of 1846).

Because of the slowness with which it arose, and its varied nature from stage to stage, Romanticism is not easily definable, except as a reaction against the reigning orthodoxies,[9] as a convenient label for an age rather than a movement, or indeed as a convenient term for one of the basic tendencies of the human spirit.[10] None of these approaches is wholly satisfactory. Thus, to confine Romanticism (as art historians tend to) to the first 30 years of the 19th century begs more questions than it answers; to see it as the antithesis of Classicism makes it seem negative (which it is not) while at the same time ignoring its frequent use of once-Classical devices and even styles.[11] To deal with Romanticism as an 'eternal' state of mind is dangerous too, for it could lead us to ignore how *timely* 18th/19th-century Romanticism actually was, and how intimately related to the changing political, industrial and social scene, not to mention philosophy, religion and various kinds of science. Thus although attempts to discern straightforward cause and effect between (for example) the French Revolution and the Lake Poets are difficult to sustain,

Romanticism was never an organised movement, with a set of commonly agreed tenets, for nothing so individualistic could ever be so. On its own, it could not hope to displace the 'Establishment' position of Classicism to become the preferred vehicle for the artistic encapsulation of State ideals; and it is tempting to view the great political upheavals of the turn of the 18th/19th centuries – the French Revolution, the Napoleonic Wars, and the subsequent Europe-wide revolutions up to and including 1848 – as both the midwife of the Romantic movement[13] and the angel of death for State Classicism.[14] Romanticism never became an 'official' style,[15] perhaps partly because it was so often heavily politicised in *opposition* to established authority and the *status quo*,[16] and partly because its complexion is bourgeois rather than aristocratic.[17] For all these reasons, Romanticism aroused strong passions at the time, and drew its crowds of attackers and defenders.[18] Political change was but one aspect of broader changes in society; and the Romantics showed themselves much more sensitive to these than had previous generations of artists or literary men.[19]

But *why* is Romanticism so difficult to define? The essence of the matter is that, unlike Classicism (which is rule-based and

L to R: William Blake, *Elohim Creating Adam,* c1795, monoprint with pen and watercolour; Henry Fuseli, *Titania and Bottom,* 1780-90, oil

there is no doubt of the liberating power of Hegel's assertion of the importance of the individual.

This account deals with Romanticism exclusively as a *movement* – and one, indeed, for which the basic literature is immense.[12] For reasons already explained, it would be unwise to try and isolate the visual arts from literature (and indeed music, were there space). Unlike Classicism, which, in the sphere of visual arts as in those of music, dance and literature, operated with a fully developed apparatus of theories, textbooks and academies, Romanticism (which operates across an equally wide range of art-forms) was completely without formal organisation. Classicism's strength was precisely in its ability to promulgate *rules* in whatever area, all based where possible on antique precedent: so that Classicism can in a sense regenerate itself and thereby maintain its important place as the provider of State art – exactly the place that significant art and architecture had enjoyed in the ancient world. Romanticism defines itself best as a series of oppositions to aspects of Classicism. Typically, the definitions tend to come after the event, rather than being prescriptive; but the characterisation of the movement by contrasting it with Classicism was adopted by A W Schlegel before 1800.

textbook-led), Romanticism is the art of the *individual*; so that artworks in whatever medium are *personal* responses to life, society and the environment. Because it is not programmatic, we cannot expect anything other than a diversity of reactions: not all Romantics are irrational, over-emotional, engrossed in landscape, medieval horror or the sublime; but their insistence on originality and individuality ensures that there can be no one Romantic 'view' of the meaning of life, or of industry, or of revolution. All in all, perhaps Romanticism is about the untramelled *diversity* of the individual human spirit rather than about the views of any particular group. Romanticism is therefore inherently *subjective*; whereas Classicism, by contrast, tends toward objectivity.

The perceived North/South division is particularly important because, although one very crucial aspect of Romanticism is that it is Europe-wide,[20] flourishing in Latin countries as well as in the North,[21] it was nevertheless acknowledged that Romanticism was born in the North – whereas Classicism was a child of the South: see the writings of, for example, Goethe. Here particularly, opposites are at work: the clear skies of the South; the mists of the North; hence the clarity and reason of the one and the dark, irrational emotionalism of the other, where reason gives way to the powers of the imagination, and sometimes to dreams and nightmares. There is, indeed, a strong strain of anti-rationalism in Romanticism – a belief that emotions and sensations can teach the individual better than all the accumulated baggage of tradition.[22] Another useful opposition, perhaps first enunciated by Goethe, is that Classicism represents health, Romanticism sickness – and he means spiritual sickness. Analogous to this is the general philosophical stance of Classicism, which is toward optimism and perfectability, based on human reason; as opposed to Romanticism's essential pessimism, which sometimes sees salvation in religion, or in emotional self-knowledge, but never in the despised platitudes of conventional social wisdom. Change was therefore not necessarily seen as *progress*. Of course, not even the Romantics always view matters in such extremes: as A W Schlegel remarks, 'Whereas reason can only comprise each object separately, feeling can perceive all in all at one and the same time.'[23] This should warn us that *consistency* is not necessarily a quality we should expect to find in Romanticism, let alone any rigid unity between form and content. Thus we can find Classical subject-matter treated

might expect from the North-South dichotomy, the focus of *geographical* attention also changes, away from the traditional Classical world of Italy and toward Africa, the Americas and the Orient, with their different cultures and art-forms.[26] Also 'rediscovered' are the under-emphasised areas of Europe itself – Greece (largely unknown since the Turkish occupation), Scotland and Wales, and the Alps and Pyrenees. All this comes under the heading of exoticism: that is, the yearning to evoke the strange and the unusual not only in landscape but also in states of mind [27] or even to express states of mind *through* landscape, as in the works of Caspar David Friedrich.

Indeed, landscape had an important role to play in Romantic art and architecture, because here again a distinction could be made between the fabricated, artificial landscape gardens of the Classicists, when Man ordered Nature (as at Chiswick House), and the beauties of natural landscape, when Man was overawed by Nature's grandeur and wildness, as with the Alps, Scotland or the English Lake District.[28] These same qualities could be used as a sounding-board for Man's emotions – for the pathetic fallacy, for religious experience, for the creation of a new kind of mythology, as in the work of Phillip Otto Runge[29] – or for the

L to R: Delacroix, *Combat of the Giaour and the Pasha Hassan*, 1856, oil; Constable, *Vale of Dedham*, 1828, oil; Géricault, *Madwoman*, oil

Romantically (Delacroix's work in the libraries of the Chamber of Deputies and the Senate, 1838-47); landscape treated apocalyptically (Turner), biblically (Samuel Palmer), or with pantheistic sentiment but in a strictly Classical form (Friedrich); contemporary subject-matter treated heroically (David and Napoleon), 'psychologically' (Géricault's portraits of the mentally ill of the early 1820s), or both at the same time (Géricault's *Raft of the Medusa* of 1819), or indeed semi-Classically (Delacroix's *Liberty at the Barricades* of 1830). In all such works, the impact is increased by the union of traditional opposites: as A W Schlegel says, 'The Romantic spirit delights in a continual *rapprochement* of the most opposite tendencies. Nature and art, poetry and prose, serious and humorous, memory and presentiment, abstract ideas and lively sensations, the divine and the terrestrial, life and death – all unite and mix in the Romantic genre.'[24]

Romanticism, Primitivism and Exoticism
Romanticism almost totally abandons the Classical past and prefers to involve itself with the primitive and the medieval, as well as with other periods, the chief attraction of all these being that they are not of the present.[25] This also means that, as one

expression of ideology, as in Constable.[30] Again, it was the appreciation (through travel and artistic representation) of actual landscape which increased the number of landscape paintings in the 19th century, helping in the process not only to destroy the tyranny of academic hierarchy, which held history painting at the top, and landscape near the bottom, but also to redefine the very boundaries of landscape painting itself.[31] It also prompted the development of Europe-wide travel. Whereas Italy had previously been the target of all desires, areas such as the Rhine and the Alps now became popular as, for example, in the paintings and prints of Turner.[32] Such travel was often professional, whether on the part of literary men or artists.[33]

If landscape was one vehicle for expressing the sensibility of the individual, then an interest in the primitive was another. Although arguably a perennial tendency in the arts,[34] primitivism is of particular importance in Romanticism, because more intimately connected with a new aesthetic sensibility and a reevaluation of earlier artistic and literary periods.[35] As well as being a way of evoking the past, primitivistic techniques were frequently used to suggest primeval simplicity (and thereby 'truth'), or emotional directness. Thus Flaxman's pseudo-Greek outline

Adrian Berg, *Sheffield Park, Autumn*, 1985-6, oil

engravings after Homer and Dante, inspired by Greek vases, are inherently no different from some of his pseudo-Gothic memorials (such as the *Agnes Cromwell*); while Blake – the embodiment of the conjunction of art and literature – conveys his message in a style usually linear, 'naive' and even 'savage'.

The Middle Ages were viewed, if not exactly as primitive, then certainly with some of the aspects attributed to primitivism, such as simplicity, honour, purity – that is, Mankind untrammelled by the dubious benefits of 'modern' civilisation, and therefore the better able to think and act in a straightforward and natural fashion.[36] Once again, such interest in the past implies a continuing alienation from the present – and provides another example of the subversive tendencies of Romanticism, perhaps first seen in the cavortings of David's followers, *les barbus*.[37] For it is possible, by acknowledging artists' 'pursuits of primitivism as the avenue to spiritual salvation',[38] to understand primitivism – no matter to what place or period it is directed – as a political and artistic critique of contemporary life.

Romanticism and modernity

'For me, Romanticism is the most recent and up-to-date expression of beauty', said Baudelaire, conscious as ever of the need for modernity in art. What Romanticism accomplished was perhaps the separation of artistic life from accumulated tradition, under the spur of contemporaneity. Indeed, one of the ways in which Romanticism expresses modernity is (perhaps surprisingly) through its very historicism – especially its abandonment of the Classical past and involvement with the primitive or the medieval – an involvement which lasts from the 18th through to the end of the 19th century.[39] The artist's attachment to the present is far from begin matter-of-fact or 'realistic', in the manner of Courbet; rather, he offers the attractions of the unbridled imagination, of sensitive reactions to the here-and-now which lift temporality toward eternity. The opportunity to do things differently is implicit in such historicism, because the new view of the past – the flowering of the new discipline of history, partly at the hands of Hegel – itself implied change.

In this sense, Romanticism is indeed a constant in European civilisation; and Romanticism *qua* movement has been a beacon for later periods, as it demonstrated one way of dealing with social, political and intellectual change – so necessary since such changes have subsequently occurred at an ever-increasing rate.

In a yet broader sense, Romanticism offered the future various ways of breaking with existing conventions. One might say that

24

Sandro Chia, *Rising Objects*, 1988, encaustic and oil

the movement loosed the bonds between subject matter and style so that, following Romanticism's example, never again could style be, as it were, 'periodised', with one style for one period. Henceforth, anything went: a whole plethora of styles can be found in any period and in any medium: the Gothic Houses of Parliament of 1836-68[40] and the Classical National Gallery of Scotland of 1850-54, with the 'industrial' Crystal Palace of 1851; or Manet's *Bar at the Folies-Bergère* of 1881-2 with Seurat's *Bathers at Asnières* of 1883-4.

In sum, what the Romantics did to traditional forms and traditional ideas changed everything permanently: there is no question of going back to where we were before the Romantics messed things up; modernity is indeed different in tone and in stance; but the changes take place in territory clearly and unalterably marked out by the preceding generations.[41] Hence the term 'Romantic' was applicable in the later 19th century, and is still of value today.[42]

Romanticism and the visual arts

Romanticism in the visual arts[43] is dependent for much of its impact on the literary or at least evocative sources the artists use. This is not to say that one needs a book by one's side in order to understand a Romantic painting, or that all Romantic paintings are particularly bookish. Rather, that full understanding of such a work can only come from appreciation of its full context. To repeat the main theme of this account, Romanticism cannot be dealt with as the expression of just one medium: to begin with, it is as we have seen first and foremost a *literary* movement rather than an artistic one. Literature, indeed, is an essential complement to any satisfactory understanding of Romantic art, not just because so many paintings are on 'literary' themes, but rather because the whole approach to the matter of art is so often a literary one by artists steeped in the works of their contemporaries and forbears. To study Constable without consulting Wordsworth, or Turner's paintings without his own poems, or Berlioz without Shakespeare, would be to miss a dimension.[44] Similarly, one cannot understand the Romantic written word without constantly being aware of the visual dimension.

Jacques Barzun believes that 'The Romantic revolution in painting was achieved by the simple means of stepping out of the studio and observing nature',[45] but this assessment surely places too much emphasis on the observation of nature rather than on the power of the natural world as a sounding board and vehicle for the artist's feelings. It also identifies Romantic painting exclusively with landscape painting, which is far from the truth. Friedrich Schlegel, writing in 1803, is closer to the mark when he characterises painting's true aim as 'not life and strength alone, but the one, incomprehensible union of soul, expression and individuality'.[46]

For Baudelaire, as we have seen, it is clear that Romanticism is not a style, any more than it depends on a particular type of subject-matter: the essence of the matter lies in *attitude* – in a point of view and a way of feeling.

As in painting and sculpture, so in architecture there is no one Romantic style, but rather a profusion of styles which complement the broadened horizons of the age. These range from the massive 'primitivism' of the early Greek Doric (inspired by the temples of Paestum and Sicily), and the exoticism of foreign styles from India and China, to a firm focus on the national architecture of the Middle Ages. The debate on the origins of Gothic began in the Romantic period;[47] but the Gothic Revival was not simply a renewed interest in ecclesiastical architecture, for secular Gothic came into vogue as well.[48] And true to the flavour of Romanticism, Gothic was an international success – surely because it was one style which answered to national(istic) needs.[49] Of all the styles of Romanticism, then, the Gothic is the most important. Although examples of Gothic (survival or revival?) can be found in the 17th century (at, for example, Cambridge), it owes its true revival to a mix of features in the 18th century: first, of course, that historicism which interested people in the Middle Ages; secondly, a parallel concern for ruins and follies, whereby time might almost be seen to be passing; and thirdly, a sensitivity to atmosphere which is also part and parcel of the vogue for landscape gardening, especially in its Picturesque phase.[50] One might say, therefore, that the interchange between literature and painting is equally palpable in architecture, where the *genius loci* and the evocative powers of the building are much more important than the mere style or materials in which it is constructed. Just as a Romantic painting or poem is intentionally evocative, so one could not adequately imbibe the flavour of a work of Romantic architecture without paying attention to the aura, provided in part by the setting, in part by the associations called to mind in the well-read spectator.

Buildings, like paintings and poems, could convey political and social messages;[51] but best of all they could convey *age* and the passing of time – ossified history, as it were. Yearning for the past, while not exclusively a Romantic obsession, is very powerful in the age of historicism; so that the 18th and early 19th centuries see a large increase in interest in ruins and decay as aesthetic foci for gardens and landscapes,[52] as for example at Fountains Abbey. By the same token the Gothic style, with its built-in 'age' and venerability, was suited to public architecture, and could sometimes be a potent element in the increasing nationalism of the 19th century,[53] although frequently it was treated as just one more style, with the industrialised Gothic re-creation of 'Gothic' objects for interior decoration, furniture and the like.[54]

Conclusion

The political and social events of the late 18th and early 19th centuries – namely the French Revolution and the Industrial Revolution – occasioned the greatest change in human life since the coming of the great world religions, or, arguably since the Neolithic revolution itself. The change was not simply a social or a political one, important as these indeed were; for it was also an intellectual and above all an emotional one, provoking different ways of looking at the human predicament – a predicament altered radically by such enormous political and social upheavals. Of course, not all was pain, introspection and trauma; for hand in hand with the destruction of the past by the Industrial Revolution went its reassessment at the hands of the new discipline of history (and its offshoot, archaeology), which led to the re-evaluation of hitherto neglected periods of the past.

Romanticism's critique of its age was both profound and longlasting. It was also essentially pessimistic, for few liked what they saw, and even fewer could ignore the (equally Romantic) conviction that life had been better in days gone by – hence the escape from the present. Above all, in contradistinction to Classicism, which had been about order and control, Romanticism tended to look at the same evidence and see despair and chaos; in Hugh Honour's words, 'The Romantics were to find that superficial appearances concealed not so much order as inpenetrable depths of inexplicable mystery'.[55]

Notes

1 cf Old French *romance*; the term has the meaning of *fabulous* in both England and France in the 17th century. J Whiteley, 'The origins and the concept of "classique" in French art criticism', *Journal of the Warburg and Courtauld Institutes* XXXXIX, 1976, pp268-75, deals also with the meaning of the word *romantic*; C Apollonio, *Romantico: storia e fortuna di una parola*, Florence, 1958; and R M Immerwarh, *Romantisch: Genese und Tradition einer Denkform*, Frankfurt, 1972. Modern usage is often very broad: J Barzun, *Romanticism and the Modern Ego*, Boston, 1943, pp213-30.

2 P Viallaneix, ed, *La Préromantisme: hypothèque ou hypothèse?* (Colloque, Clermont Ferrand, 1972 Paris, 1975, especially pp9ff; B Hepworth, *The Rise of Romanticism: Essential Texts*, Manchester, 1978.

3 G Hoffmeister, *Deutsche und Europaische Romantik*, Stuttgart, 1978; W Vaughan, *German Romantic Painting*, New Haven, 1980; F Cummings, 'Romanticism and Britain, 1760-1860', pp17-24, in F Cummings & A Staley, eds, *Romantic Art in Britain: Paintings and Drawings 1760-1860* (exhibition catalogue), Philadelphia 1968.

4 L Reynaud, *Le romantisme: ses origines anglogermaniques, influences étrangères et traditions nationales, le réveil du génie français*, Paris, 1926; L R Furst, *Romanticism in Perspective: A Comparative Study of Aspects of the Romantic Movements in England, France and Germany*, London, 1969; J G Robertson, *Studies in the Genesis of Romantic Theory in the Eighteenth Century*, Cambridge, 1923, for the primacy of Italy.

5 W Vaughan, *German Romanticism and English Art*, New Haven, 1979;

A D Potts, 'British Romantic Art Through German Eyes', in *Sind Briten hier?: Relations between British and Continental Art 1680-1880*, Munich, 1981, pp181-205.

6 J Koerner, *Die Botschaft der Deutschen Romantik an Europa*, Augsburg 1929.

7 F Brie, *Egotismus der Sinne, Eine Studie zur Psychologie der Romantik*, Heidelberg, 1920, pp5-17.

8 G Thurley, *The Romantic Predicament*, London, 1983, pp45.

9 J B Halsted, *Romanticism: Problems of Definition, Explanation, and Evaluation*, Boston, 1968; H Peyre, *What is Romanticism?*, Eng trans, Alabama, 1977.

10 F L Lucas, *The Decline and Fall of the Romantic Ideal*, 3rd ed, Cambridge, 1963, ch II, and p139: 'The pure Classic is too stiff and stifled; the pure Romantic too drunken and wayward; the pure Realist too drab; the Surrealist a self-segregated sot. Classicism, Romanticism, Realism are three extremes, three points of a triangle; the magic circle lies inscribed within it.'

11 A K Wiedmann, *Romantic Roots in Modern Art: Romanticism and Expressionism: A Study in Comparative Aesthetics*, Woking, 1979, p54ff.

12 J Dobai, *Die Kunstliteratur des Klassizismus und der Romantik in England*, Bern, 3 Vols, 1974, 1975, 1977; D H Reiman, *English Romantic Poetry, 1800-1835: A Guide to Information Sources*, Detroit, 1979; A C Elkins and L J Forstner, eds, *The Romantic Movement Bibliography, 1936-1970*, a master cumulation from *ELH, Philological Quarterly* and *English Language Notes*, 7 vols, Ann Arbor, Mich, 1973; *Romantisme: Revue de la Société des Etudes Romantiques*, Paris, p197ff; *Les annales romantiques:*

revue d'histoire du romantisme, Paris, 1904-14; *The Romantic Movement: A Bibliographical Supplement to English Language Notes*, 1964-1978.

13 See generally *French Painting 1774-1830: The Age of Revolution*, exhibition, Paris, Detroit, New York, 1974-5; and H M Jones, *Revolution & Romanticism*, Cambridge, Mass, 1974. and specifically A de Paz, *La rivoluzione romantica: poetiche, estetiche, ideologie*, Naples, 1984, p37ff; and R Paulson, Representations of Revolution (1789-1820), New Haven, 1983.

14 M Greenhalgh, *The Classical Tradition in Art*, London, 1978, pp225-33: 'Ingres and the Subversion of the Classical Tradition'; K Clark, *The Romantic Rebellion: Romantic versus Classic Art*, London, 1973.

15 K Kroeber, *British Romantic Art*, Berkeley, 1986, discusses the 'provocat ions' of Romantic art and why, despite its liberating and invigorating effects, Romantic art was so quickly challenged and inverted by Victorian and early modern art.

16 E E Nower, *The Artist as Politician: The Relationship between the Art and the Politics of the French Romantic Literary and Artistic Figures*, Berkeley, 1975; C C Brinton, *The Political Ideas of the English Romanticists*, New York, 1926; A Joussain, *Romantisme et politique*, Paris, 1924; *Romantique et politique*, Paris, 1969; H Honour, *Romanticism*, London, 1979; W Vaughan, *Romantic Art*, London, 1979, ch 6.

17 cf F Antal, 'Reflections on Classicism and Romanticism', in his *Classicism and Romanticism*, London, 1966, pp1-45.

18 eg E Bellorini, *Discussioni e polemiche sul romanticismo*, 1816-1826, reedited by A M Mutterle, Bari, 1975; R A Foakes, *Romantic Criticism 1800-1850*, 1968.

19 cf A D Harvey, *English Poetry in a Changing Society*, 1780-1825, London, 1980; and R W Harris, *Romanticism and the Social Order*, 1780-1830, London, 1969. But for the view that Romanticism is predominantly a psychological, *not* a sociological phenomenon, cf A Rodway, *The Romantic Conflict*, London, 1963.

20 L R Furst, *The Contours of European Romanticism*, London, 1979; L R Furst, ed, *European Romanticism: Self-Definition, An Anthology*, London, 1980; P Van Tieghem, *L'ère romantique: le romantisme dans la littérature européenne*, 2nd ed with excellent (and updated) bibliographies, Paris, 1969.

21 eg A Farinelli, *Il romanticismo nel mondo latino*, 3 vols, Turin, 1927, vol 3 being a wide-ranging bibliographical survey.

22 M Praz, *The Romantic Agony*, Eng trans, London, 1970; G Briganti, *I pittori dell'immaginario: arte e rivoluzione psicologica*, Milan, 1977, for the topic from Fuseli and Blake to Boecklin and de Chirico; U Bode, *Kunst zwischen Traum und Alptraum: phantastische Malerei im 19 Jahrhundert*, Braunschweig, 1981.

23 Cited in Wiedman, p12. See also, *op cit*, p13ff. for 'the retreat from reason'.

24 A W Schlegel, *Vorlesungen VI*, p161ff. cf R W Ewton, *The Literary Theories of A W Schlegel*, The Hague/Paris, 1972, pp 99-106.

25 C Duncan, *The Pursuit of Pleasure: The Rococo Revival in French Romantic Art*, New Haven, 1976.

26 eg M Taha-Hussein, *Le romantisme français et l'Islam*, Dar Al-Maare, 1962.

27 Brie, *op cit*, pp21-70, for exoticism in English and French literature.

28 L Hawes, *Presences of Nature: British Landscape*, 1780-1830, New Haven, 1982.

29 O G von Simson, 'Phillip Otto Runge and the Mythology of Landscape', *AB* XXIV, 1942, p335: 'he realised earlier and more clearly than any other artist that landscape was the great mythological experience of the 19th century.'

30 A Bermingham, *Landscape and Ideology: The English Rustic Tradition*, 1740-1860, Berkeley, 1986.

31 R Paulson, *Literary Landscape: Turner and Constable*, London, 1982.

32 G Dischner, *Ursprünge der Rheinromantik in England: zur Geschichte der romantischen Aesthetik*, Frankfurt, 1972 (in series *Studien zur Philosophie und Literatur des 19 Jahrhunderts*, no 17); F-M Tsigakou, *The Rediscovery of Greece: Travellers and Painters of the Romantic Era*, London, 1981; T Webb ed, *English Romantic Hellenism*, 1700-1824, New York, 1982; E Skasa-Weiss, *Bergromantik in der Malerei des 19 Jahrhunderts*, Munich, 1977.

33 M S R Morrill, *The British Literary Traveller on the Continent, 1795 to 1825*, PhD Thesis, New York University, 1976; J-U Fechner, *Erfahrene und erfundene Landschaft. Aurelio de' Giorgi Bertolas Deutschlandbild und die Begründung der Rheinromantik*, Opladen, 1974.

34 E H Gombrich, 'The Primitive and its Value in Art', four talks reprinted in *The Listener*, 15 Feb, 22 Feb, 1 March and 8 March 1979.

35 M Curtis (text and cat), Levitine, (introduction), *Search for Innocence: Primitive and Primitivistic Art of the Nineteenth Century*, exhibition, University of Maryland Art Gallery, 1975; S Sulzberger, *La réhabilitation des primitifs flamands* 1802-67 (Académie royale de Belgique: Classe des Beaux-Arts: mémoires XII fasc 3), Brussels, 1961. Superville is a key figure of B M Stafford, *Symbol and Myth: Humbert de Superville's Essay on Absolute Signs in Art*, London, 1979.

36 A Chandler, *A Dream of Order: The Medieval Ideal in Nineteenth-Century English Literature*, Lincoln, Nebraska, 1970.

37 G Levitine, *The Dawn of Bohemianism: The Barbu Rebellion and Primitivism in Neoclassical France*, London, 1978: the first organised and deliberate alienation from society by a group of artists in the modern age.

38 Wiedmann, 1979, *op cit*, p240.

39 eg J Banham & J Harris, eds, *William Morris and the Middle Ages*, Whitworth Art Gallery, Manchester, 1984; R Lanson, *Le goût de Moyen Age en France au XVIIIe siècle*, Paris/Brussels, 1926.

40 M H Port, ed, *The Houses of Parliament*, New Haven, 1976.

41 Thurley, 1983, *op cit*, p89; C Rosen & H Zerner, *Romanticism and Realism: The Mythology of Nineteenth-Century Art*, New York, 1984.

42 D Mellor, ed, *Paradise Lost: The Neo-Romantic Imagination in Britain 1935-55*, Exhibition, Barbican Art Gallery, London, 1987; R Rosenblum, *Modern Painting and the Northern Romantic Tradition: Friedrich to Rothko*, New York, 1975; G C Hough, *The Last Romantics*, London, 1961 (studies of Ruskin, Rossetti, Morris, Pater, Whistler and Yeats).

43 Surveys in J Clay, *Romanticism*, Eng trans New York, 1981; M Le Bris, *Romantics and Romanticism*, Eng trans, Geneva, 1981; P Courthion, *Romanticism*, Eng trans, Geneva.

44 J A W Hefferman, *The Re-creation of Landscape: A Study of Wordsworth, Coleridge, Constable and Turner*, London, 1984, pp54-102: 'The displacement of history'. More generally, W Rasch, ed, *Bildende Kunst und Literatur: Beiträge zum Problem ihrer Wechselziehungen im neunzehnten* Frankfurt, 1970 (*Studien zur Philosophie und Literatur des 19 Jahrhunderts*, no 6), especially K K Polheim, 'Die romantische einheit der Künstë', pp157-78; and Raabe, 'Dichterverherrlichung im neunzehnten Jahrhundert. Zum Anteil der Bildenden Kunst an der Darstellung der Literaturgeschichte', pp79-101.

45 J Barzun, *Romanticism and the Modern Ego*, Boston, 1943, pp88.

46 Cited in Honour, 1979, *op cit*, p127.

47 J Frew, 'An Aspect of the Early Gothic Revival: The Transformation of Medievalist Research, 1770-1800', *Journal of the Warburg and Courtauld Institutes* XLIII, 1980.

48 S Lang, 'The Principles of the Gothic Revival in England', *Journal of the Society of Architectural Historians* XXV.4, 1966; C L Eastlake, *A History of the Gothic Revival*, ed and introduction J Mordaunt Crook, New York, 1970; J Macaulay, *The Gothic Revival, 1743-1845*, Glasgow, 1975 – for Scotland and the North of England; T Davis, *The Gothick Taste*, Newton Abbot, 1974.

49 G Germann, *Gothic Revival in Europe and Britain: Sources, Influences and Ideas*, Eng trans, London, 1972; A Meyer, *Neugotik und Neuromantik in der Schweiz: Die Kirchenarchitektur des 19 Jahrhunderts*, Zurich, 1975; Schneider, ed, Berlin, *Bauwerke der Neugotik*, Berlin, 1984.

50 Dischner, 1972, *op cit*, p37ff.

51 G Eimer, *Quellen zur politischen Ikonographie der Romantik: SteinsTurmbau in Nassau* (Frankfurter Fundamente der Kunstgeschichte II, Kunstgeschichtliches Institut der Johann Wolfgang Goethe-Universität), Frankfurt, 1987.

52 G Hartinann, *Die Ruine im Landschaftsgarten: Ihre Bedeutung für den frühen Historismus und die Landschaftsmalerei der Romantik*, Worms, 1981; Zucker, *Fascination of Decay, Ruins: Relic – Symbol – Ornament*, Ridgewood, NJ, 1968; R Mortier, *La Poétique des ruines en France: ses origines, ses variations de la Renaissance à Victor Hugo*, Geneva, 1974.

53 N Pevsner, *Ruskin and Viollet-le-Duc: Englishness and Frenchness in the Appreciation of Gothic Architecture*, London, 1969; G L Hersey, *High Victorian Gothic: A Study in Associationism*, Baltimore, 1972.

54 L Grodecki intro, *Le 'gothique' retrouvé avant Viollet-le-Duc*, Paris, 1979.

55 Honour, 1979, *op cit*, p34.

———— * ————

Thérèse Oulton, *Sleeper*, 1987, oil

CONCEPTS OF ROMANTICISM
John Griffiths

Markus Lüpertz, *Nude with Melon (Courbet)*, 1985, oil

'Romanticism' is a highly problematical term in discourse about art. Historians of ideas treat it warily even when examining its use in a specific historical context. Art critics use it impressionistically, if at all, in occasional pieces in which the occasion defines the concept. Nevertheless increasing talk of the 'new Romanticism' in relation to contemporary European and even American painting indicates some kind of implicit agreement about certain constants in art and its

contexts for which 'Romanticism' is still the only appropriate notion. A short survey offers some ideas about the term's utility now. Classicism and Romanticism, in so far as they can be defined apart from a definite culture, time and place, and apart from specific works of art, are two essential aspects of human nature. Even though sometimes the connection is very tenuous indeed, this fundamental human experience of contraries lies behind all but the most perverse instances of Classical-Romantic opposition in the history of ideas, literature, the visual arts, and so on. In this sense, the Classical-Romantic antithesis existed before and during the disputes between 'Ancients' and 'Moderns' in antiquity (between the supporters of Homer and those of Callimachus in ancient Alexandria, for instance); before the often acrimonious divide between the old and the new cultures in 12th-century Italy; and before the early 19th-century association of Romanticism with political revolution and the release of the individual conceived as an autonomous and uniquely creative social and sexual being, equally entitled to self-assertion alongside other beings (Classicism was linked to the restoration of political, ecclesiastical and cultural order and uniformity).

This basic human antithesis underlies a number of fundamental aesthetic and artistic oppositions such as the Aristotelian contrast between form and matter, or Schiller's between 'naive' and 'sentimental' literature, to mention only two from a vast list of relevant possibilities.

In art Romantics may be thought of then as a constant, or set of associated constants, related to the Romantic psychological disposition, with its anti-conformism, preference for spontanei-

ty, the sudden inspired impression, and vibrant, even violent colour rather than perfect finish and line. It indicates a passionate desire to exceed limits, a longing for liberty, an overreaching without anxious scrutiny of the bounds of love and passion.

The Romantic is then a preference for a certain kind of configuration before the figure; a culturally inherited schema or *eidos* which reinforces a genetically inherited disposition. As time passes, and given some agreement about the persistence of a shared civilisation (in this case the Graeco-Roman, Judaeo-Christian West) which allows any talk of tradition and of course the possibility of revolt, breakaway and innovation, acknowledged examples of Romanticism constitute a reserve of themes and tropes. Thus a 'Romantic tradition' which can be transmitted and cited comes into being. It remains meaningful not only because it is an historically established system of norms which can be activated by bored artists or critics who want a name for their whims, but because it still corresponds to something basic in our shared experience.

Although Classicism and Romanticism are not scientific terms, it is not fanciful to claim that they correspond to certain clusters of observable traits discussed in 20th-century theories of psychological types, for instance, the Jungian contrast of conscious, intellectual, rational types with unconscious, instinctual, emotional types is clearly related to the authentic Classical-Romantic opposition.

Modern theories of personality which admit the notion of types and 'component' traits naturally see them as existing in various mixtures in individuals, and to some extent in significant works of art produced by such persons. Theories of personality from Hippocrates in ancient Greece through Galen down to Kant were theories of temperament which for the most part conceived of an individual as of this temperament, profoundly associated with all others of the same temperament, but opposed to all other individuals variously disposed in the categories of those other three temperaments. A person and all that was characteristic of a person was either choleric or sanguine or phlegmatic or melancholic. Wundtian and associated personality theory in the 14th century was more nuanced. Though the non-emotional type, for example, was one person, and the emotional type was another, cross-categorical dimensions seemed more apposite to human reality than unassailable compartments. People could be 'changeable' and 'unchangeable'. Admixtures were possible.

Until the era of Wundt, however, works of art seen as expressions of their authors were often conceived as of this or that temperament or type, as were 'characters' depicted in literature or painting. In various ways the old Galenic-Kantian notion of distinct temperaments made human self-consciousness categorical. It entered into the creative process,

a Lie & a Deceit, to say the least of it. For if it is a Deceit, the whole Bible is Madness. This Opinion originates in the Greeks calling the Muses daughters of Memory. The Enquiry in England is not whether a Man has Talents & Genius, But whether he is Passive & Polite & a virtuous Ass & obedient to Noblemen's Opinions in Art & Science . . . I do not believe that Rafael taught Mich. Angelo, or that Mich. Angleo taught Rafael . . . I do not believe the tales of Anecdote writers when they militate against Individual character.'

The various academic and scholarly ideas of 'Classical' and 'Romantic' at different times and in different countries have often interacted with and sometimes coincided with the accepted categories of temperament or dimensions of personality. Moreover, though Classical and Romantic attitudes in the sense of fundamental aspects of human nature are opposed they may coexist in opposition in the same person or work ('Without contraries there is no progression' – Blake). On the other hand, a work may be wholly given over to one or the other. Local traditions, of course, can vary the tendency. Commonsense, for instance, is a variety of Classicism often met with in the British cultural tradition; it turns to satire when it specialises in the

L to R: Francesco Goya, *Prison Scene*, c1808-12, oil; William Blake, *Pity*, c1795, monoprint, pen and watercolour

and survived into the early and middle Romantic periods. The temperaments were minimally rehandled to satisfy new interest in, say, phrenology, the study of the expressions of criminals, of the insane and of 'characteristic' or psychologically totemic animals. They were superficially redefined to accord with the exotic comparative anthropology made possible by proficient voyages to the dwelling-places of 'natural' and 'primitive' man, and with archaeological finds. Careful, all-but-scientific record-keeping for various activities, from such voyages and digs to refined anatomy and study of the deranged, eventually made more exact distinctions necessary. When T G Wainewright – artist, connoisseur and poisoner transported to Van Diemen's Land – remarked in 1820 of Fuseli's 'strained' postures: 'This great genius generally selects his subjects from the traditions of early barbarous times, when men freely obeyed the fierce impulses of their nature, when their passions were undisguised and naked as their forms', he was at the point when our particular modern apprehension of 'Romanticism' in relation to art was becoming explicit.

The same trend appears in Blake: 'Reynold's Opinion was that Genius May Be Taught & that all Pretence to Inspiration is

exposure and ridicule of absurd, affected and sentimental behaviour. Strange to say, in the face of its wit and elegant fantasy, Romanticism tends to become highly serious and self-regarding.

In the most basic sense, however, Romanticism beyond national boundaries, in ideas, literature and art, has exploited the human tendency to 'instinctive', 'emotional' expression which seeks to overrun all boundaries. The Romantic consciousness sees itself as unique, and 'He knows himself greatly who never opposes his genius' (Lavater). The Romantic artist rises above mundane reality because marked out from birth – or, preferably, from eternity. The artist-seer '. . . by the vision splendid/Is on his way attended' (Wordsworth, 'Immortality Ode'). And 'every artist has, or ought to have, a character or system of his own; if, instead of referring that to the test of nature, you judge him by your own packed notions, or arraign him at the tribunal of schools which he does not recognise – you degrade the dignity of art, and add another fool to the herd of Dilettanti' (Fuseli).

The Romantic-being first communes with self: 'Do not conceal from me thy secret recesses . . . Know, my heart, that no friendship is wiser and more abounding in blessings, than the friendship and intimacy of a heart with itself' (Lavater). But after sufficient self-communing, it longs for something greater than itself to assuage the fierce delights and tender torture of uniqueness. Wordsworth's wanderer must dedicate himself to search from eve to morn, 'But doubly pitying Nature loves to show'r/Soft on his wounded heart her healing pow'r.' Shelley's Alastor must quit his 'alienated home' and travel he know not where, 'To seek strange truths in undiscovered lands'.

Romanticism always tries to maintain and develop by any means available the particular self-consciousness of the naturally privileged individual becoming aware of his or her uniqueness (we are all unique; but for a variety of reasons not all of us are aware of self; and many who are aware, not to the same degree). The special myth of nearly all cultural Romantics is that the Romantic consciousness is ever in search of its totality: of that, as it were, empyrean realm in which its uniqueness will find completion. The Romantic urge is to connect or reconcile its special individuality through ideas, or literature, or art, with nature; or with reality; or with the totality of things. So strong is this urge, yet so contrary to its yearning are private and social circumstances, that it is also typically Romantic to be passionately awry; 'The Engines in Fuseli's Mind are Blasphemy,

with nature, and even nature with nature, for the fissure runs through all that is.

This trend in painting is often most obvious in Romantic landscape, as in Caspar David Friedrich, and in many 'descriptions' of landscape in verse in which complex psychological processes of exploration of the growing spirit within are enacted in terms of the landscape without, and a far from simple reconciliation of human subject and nature-as-object appears to have been made – Wordsworth's *Prelude* is the best example of this.

Nevertheless, though there are many depictions of Romantic longing in symbolic and allegorical landscapes, it would be ridiculous in the contemporary English fashion to restrict the Romantic tradition in painting to landscape, and to find its best instances in a spurious English descent from the late 18th century to the present day, from Constable's *Dedham Vale*, say, to those of Moore's sculptures that were established upon the appearance and feel of a unique found object – smooth stone or weathered wood – which transmitted to the new creation some part of the maker's experience of a solitary conspiracy with nature. Fuseli's *Nightmare*, for example, is a soulscape which relates agonised self-consciousness to sexuality and heightened

 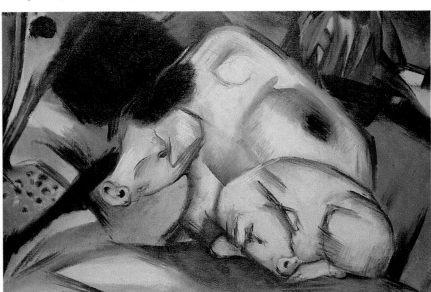

L to R: Ernst Ludwig Kirchner *Semi-Nude Woman in a Hat*, 1911, oil; Franz Marc, *pigs*, 1926, oil

lechery and blood. His women are all whores and men all banditti. They are whores not from the love of pleausure but from a hatred, a malignant spite against virtue, and his men are not villains from a daring desire or wish, but a licentious turbulence' (B R Haydon).

The Romantic ambition is to be complete, to repair the deficiencies of our present incomplete state in that other state towards which the wistful characters in Caspar David Friedrich's landscapes direct their gaze, aided by symbols of hope, giant optic glasses provided by nature: the arc of the rainbow at whose centre man is poised to peer through the cloudy sky beyond; the white rocks that crack to allow a human trinity a vision of ineffable light over the disappearing sea, which lies at first sight beyond but then below. The window-shutter is open to allow a vision of the other world with its marker mast of hope; it casts light back (so it seems) into the bleak interior emblematic of the hitherto self-communing if not self-sufficient soul – which longs for union and enlightenment (eg *Landscape with Rainbow*, 1809; *White Rocks above Rügen*, 1819; *Woman at a Window*, 1822). This reconciliation of self and nature may also bring about a cosmic or even universal reconciliation of imagination

states of mind and body, and contains enough elements of non-Romantic tradition to differentiate new from old. But the absence of torrents, cliffs, clouds, rainbows, mountains, and of other emblems of natural exaltation with which the exaltation within the individual feels affinity, does not disqualify the *Nightmare* from Romantic status.

The interactions of even the most important Romantic traditions in art and literature across Europe are so varied and paradoxical as to defy such tedious restrictions. The mysterious cathedrals which the individuals in the foreground of a Schinkel painting or print seek and espy through a great enveloping tree, or the ruined cloister glimpsed through an accommodating rock in Blechen's painting, *The Ruined Monastery* (1828), or Goya's *Madhouse Yard* (1793) and Géricault's *Study of a Kleptomaniac* (1822), in their depiction of extreme and privileged states of being within and without, are as 'Romantic' as Palmer's *In a Shoreham Garden* (1829) or Constable's *Dedham Vale* (1828).

Romantic emphases differed with the rise and fall of individual artists and schools, but above all with major political events. The French Romanticism sanctioned by the Revolution was somewhat unlike German and British models. It followed the Rights of Man and stressed a more political form of individual freedom, which the thinkers, *littérateurs* and artists of revolution had to define. They succeeded so well that Romantic notions in France passed into the everyday self-consciousness. One such was that art was a form of excess, of justifiable soaring beyond the normal bounds of still-fettered humankind ('. . . the sublime eagles and big birds of the French Academy fly up far beyond the sphere of our affections' – Samuel Palmer). So it seemed to the heirs of the revolution who looked to its origins in the work of the philosophers of Enlightenment, and to the prophets of the apotheosis of Natural Man, like Rousseau.

The French Romantics were also exotic; they sought out appositely lustrous oriental and even noble and mysterious medieval models – though here one of the great paradoxes of Romanticism began which still haunts it; for the Middle Ages represented the dreamtime of the *ancien régime* and of the papacy, which saw the unbridled individualism of the revolt of 1789 and of the declaration of 1791 as the culmination of a line of rebellion and anarchism that had started with the Protestant Reformation.

French Romantics were also egalitarian: the subject-matter of

tending into the future (or of the Restoration, extending into the medieval past). Instead, and in spite of such obeissances to democratic sentiment as Adolph von Menzel's painting of the funeral of the '*Marzgefallenen*' – those who had fallen in the March uprising of 1848 – German artists liked to see themselves more as agents of all history questing for its fulfilment.

Imagination was an artist's privileged land where he could undertake the long quest for the great goal. Reconciliation with woman, the earth, nature, the home or the homeland was a favoured theme. In Hegel's *Phenomenology of Spirit*, in Wordsworth's *Prelude*, and in the paintings of Friedrich and his followers, the individual is in quest of a unity from which he or she has been severed – and for one school of German artists that also meant national unity. The cultivation of the unique imagination, shown in terms of insertion into a sublimely extensive but eventually welcoming landscape, was a major Romantic theme. The natural polarity of the sublime and the fair was seen as educative, as were all those landscapes of the passionately contemplative mind fed by study of nature: 'Fair seed-time had my soul, and I grew up/Foster'd alike by beauty and by fear' (*The Prelude*). For some English artists whose work offered

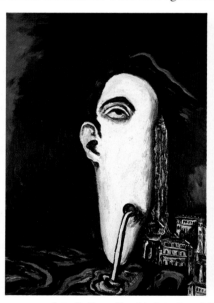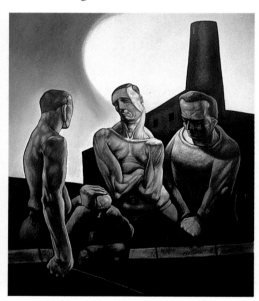

L to R: Enzo Cucchi, *Intoxicated Fountain*, 1982, oil; Ken Currie, *Boys' Night Out*, 1988, oil; Peter Howson, *Prison Scene*, 1988, oil

literature and art could come from all social classes, and here indeed the 'hero of the people' and the noble proletarian were grafted on to the older Christian theme of the Suffering Servant (eg Vernet's *The Soldier Labourer*, 1822). The same interest confronts us in much contemporary Glaswegian painting. Unlike Romantics elsewhere, French artists also wanted an audience of as many people as possible from various social levels. Accordingly, they often played down esoteric, intellectually paradoxical elements and played up populist longings. Imaginative creation and lovemaking were analogous ways of access to the special experience and to grand originality, and featured as themes of some French Romantic art as well as literature. But social reform was more important than the reconciliation with the ultimate represented in the symbolic landscapes of English and German artists.

German Romantics, apart from a flirtation with Napoleonic France during the French occupation which affected even Goethe's and Hegel's good judgement (for Hegel, Napoleon was 'the World Spirit on horseback'), were not very interested in the rights of man, populist sentiment, and so on. They did not conceive themselves as the avant-garde of the Revolution ex-

astounding and terrible prospects of vast echoing landscape within the conscience and ever-spiralling spirit, such as John Martin with his hellscapes, it was not so much external nature as the bible and associated classics such as Bunyan and Milton which offered inspiration.

By the mid-century all the foregoing tendencies had received full and varied expression as war and revolution succeeded one another. The never-ending series of discoveries in the natural sciences and in hitherto quasi-scientific fields such as psychology, together with several versions of evolutionary theory and devastating biblical criticism, brought Romanticism to the point of greatest cultural strain. But the peculiar threats and uncertainties of new thought also made it the most appropriate source of innovation.

Probably the first cultural exposition of what amounted to Classical and Romantic in a way which combined philosophic, scholarly and psychological concepts was Nietzsche's in *The Birth of Tragedy out of the Spirit of Music* (1872). The Nietzschean example is especially important, for in a pure state, but more often in adulterated, hearsay forms, it affected and continues to affect a vast number of writers and artists as well as cultural pundits. It soon became part of the self-conception of a large number of educated modern artists in continental Europe. Nietzsche (in his oblique and richly paradoxical way – itself highly modern) defined major aspects of modern art which quite distinguish it from the art of previous epochs: the connection between dissonance and the tragic impulse, for instance. He did so within the framework of a Classical-Romantic opposition that, apart from certain obviously local features, is still essentially characteristic of, say, 1970s-80s German and Italian new figurative painting and 1980s Glasgow figuration – to cite some examples of contemporary art often termed 'Romantic'.

At the beginning of *The Birth of Tragedy* Nietzsche describes the 'continuous development of art' as bound up with the Apollonian and Dionysian duality: 'Just as procreation depends on the duality of the sexes, involving perpetual strife with only periodically intervening reconciliations. The terms Dionysian and Apollonian we borrow from the Greeks, who disclose to the discerning mind the profound mysteries of their view of art, not, to be sure, in concepts, but in the impressively clear figures of their gods'. In the Greek world, Nietzsche says, there was a sharp opposition between the Apollonian art of sculpture and

able and discordant parts.

Dionysus is dismembered universal man who recalls a time when all was one and longs for a return to that consummate unity: 'art is the joyous hope that the bonds of individuation may be broken in augury of a restored oneness'. Dionysian, 'Romantic' art, therefore, has a reintegrative function. In order to reach the desired state of psychological oneness with other human beings and with nature, the artist must pass through a phase of Dionysian intoxication, of strenuous artistic endeavour before art is sublated and becomes unnecessary in a time of universal human fulfilment.

Nietzsche's was the up-to-date version of the Romantic impulse in late 19th-century and early 20th-century aesthetics. For reasons unknown (there are many disparate suggestions why), the spread of Nietzschean ideas coincided with the 'wild' or Fauvist painting of first Gauguin then Matisse, orientalist ecstasies in Diaghilev's *Ballets Russes* and the *décors* and costumes of Bakst, the explorations of aberrant and bizarre sexuality and states of mind in the prints of Max Klinger, and in the black and white drawings of Beardsley for the process block (*Under the Hill*, *The Rape of the Lock*, or the flagellant frontispiece to John

L to R: Markus Lüpertz, *Babylon Dithyrambic II*, 195, oil; K H Hödicke, *The Island of the Dead, 1986, oil; Georg Baselitz, Red Brick*

the non-plastic art of music. In Attic tragedy the long antagonism of the two inimical principles was somehow resolved. The Apollonian art-world may be seen as one of the artistic rehandling of life in graceful form and play, harmonious epic and contented anticipatory dreams. In the controlled, shining light of Apollo the inner world of fantasy is held in philosophical calm, preserved from interference from the wilder emotions. Opposed to it is the Dionysian art-world of music, fruitfulness, ecstasy and strenuousness; of chaos, drunkenness and unleashed passions.

The Romantic being must recognise the longing within him of the goat-man (once torn limb from limb by Maenads) to leave humdrum bourgeois calm to substitute passionate commitment for consciously worked and imposed schemes of order; and by becoming elemental to unite himself with the elements. Apollonian order has been imposed on the seething Dionysian chaos 'below', which is fundamental to man. Apollo is the sign of individuality in the mere appearance of things; the superficial human world, satisfied to remain calm at the price however of a divided individuality – both dividing people from one another and dividing the innermost being of each person into irreconcil-

Davidson's satirical novel about bizarre contemporary intellectual fashions, *The Strange Adventures of Earl Lavander*). Beardsley was seen by contemporaries as showing poignantly that, 'Nowadays the life of the individual is for the most part robbed of its profound inner value by the pressures of our civilisation, by the city, by the inadequate capacity of the nervous system which our generation has inherited' (Hermann Esswein, *Aubrey Beardsley*, Munich, 1912). Bakst's exotic designs for 'L'aprés-midi d'un Faune' (1912), the suggestions of Dionysian excess, wild, exaggerated movement and fierce colour contrasts in those for *Shéhérezade* and *Narcisse*, reflect the then novel liberation of primitive sensuality and primordial instinct which it was beauty's responsibility to sanction. These and similar works, more than any landscape painting, were authentic artistic expressions of the development of Romanticism typified by Nietzsche.

The symbolist Expressionism of Marc, the orientalism of Macke, the wild colour of Kirchner and the Blaue Reiter group were also indebted, *inter alia*, to late German Romanticism.

By the 1960s, and with the student movement of 1968-70, the particular set of 'Romantic' interests developed in the early 19th

Joseph Beuys, *Lightning*, 1982-5, bronze

century by Schiller, Novalis, Hegel and others, with its anti-scientism and anti-empiricism, and its constant stress on yearning for a restored harmony of man and nature, had absorbed the influences of Freudian and other depth psychologies and a largely non-Stalinist or 'Romantic' marxism. It emerged in the highly-nuanced 'critical theory' of the Frankfurt School of Social Research. After exile in the USA during the Hitler years, the most subtle theorists of the School, Theodor Adorno and Max Horkheimer, had returned to teach in Germany. The less-subtle Herbert Marcuse spread similar ideas in the USA. Like notions were also active in the lectures and works of associated sociologists and philosophers of a new generation, such as Jürgen Habermas and Albrecht Wellmer. Students of the humanities and the arts throughout Germany and in many centres elsewhere responded enthusiastically, even fanatically, to a number of ideas extrapolated from the theory. Above all, the old Romantic anti-scientism now appeared as anti-positivism, anti-behaviourism, and as a critique of the entire Enlightenment tradition that seemed to permit a benevolent yet repressive system of education. The systems of East and West were interrogated for their actual repression and 'repressive tolerance'.

These ideas 'in the air' affected more than one generation of artists, and are especially apparent – obliquely yet definitely – in the 'new painting' of Markus Lüpertz, Georg Baselitz, Bernd Koberling, K H Hödicke, A R Penck and associates. The large, bold, monumental style, combining critique, memorial and forward-looking assertiveness, the heavy adventurous inscriptions into the void, the critical references to monuments and militaristic symbols, and in the case of Penck to Eastern repressiveness, shared a common distrust of *belle peinture*, the academy and 'the system'. They rejected tedious forms of artistic order and calm ('academic ruminants' – Nietzsche) inappropriate to the times, such as the remnants of Op Art, while stopping short of Conceptualism. They were among the most serious of the 'New Romantics'. The Italian and Scottish equivalents offered similar evidence of a critique of repression and stuffiness, and a yearning for a harmony personal, social and artistic. But here artists have tempered or extended, or lightened the Germanic versions with local references. The ecstatic, rumbustious extra-Dionysian aspect was stressed by Chia and the Italians; the heroic, self-regarding artist as representative clown by Wiszniewski and similar Scottish artists.

It was a Conceptualist (of sorts) who proffered the widest-ranging set of Romantic attitudes. Joseph Beuys took the desire to reconcile nature with aberrant humankind into a 'Direct Democracy' movement and espousal of the Green political and environmentalist cause. His 'actions' and 'happenings' included tree-planting and symbolic street sweeping. He took the critique of the academy to the extent of making his dismissal from a Düsseldorf teaching post part of his Romantic stance. Some of the themes he celebrated and interrogated in his sculptural projects showed him as another Dionysus suffering symbolically. His yearning for the steppes and the primal tundra, for the primordial forest and unpolluted soil, for the magical hares and nomad tribes, for primal substances such as fat and fur, were more Romantic gestures than chance elements of his rescue by Tartars who wrapped him in fat and felt when he was shot down over the Russian Front in World War II.

The shaman's stripes and branches from the ur-*Wald* of a typical early 1980s Beuys installation reveal, more clearly than many devices in monumental painting of the same period in Germany and elsewhere, the equivocal Romantic antecedents of the tendency. The benevolent blood-and-soil philosophy, the desire for the simple tribal and folk community, the mystique of the forest and the liking for magical greenery, pine branches and the Celtic-Teutonic hare, remind us that Romanticism in its Dionysian version has dangerous possibilities. The longing for reconciliation may, after all, be born of a very exclusivist collaboration with ultimate destiny. Like all contemporary heroic Romanticism in European art, Beuys drew on some of the same aspirations exploited by Nazism. The possibility of equivocation is never absent from much Romanticist work of the 1970s-80s.

In the present, 'pluralist' situation of Western art the self-distrust and irony of, for example, early Modernism, Dadaism and Beckmannian Expressionism continue in a more heightened form. They are discernible in a comprehensive 'ensemblist' form of attack and interrogation that turns conflict and paradox into a sufficient positive. In so far as artists heed art-talk and quasi-philosophic discourse, they are influenced by the intellectual mood signalled by, say, Deleuze's post-Nietzschean uncertainty and Derrida's Deconstructionism. This trend is encouraged by the visual equivalent 'romantic irony': Irving Babbitt's term for the centrifugal viewpoint, the facing-both-ways of Romantic relativism which almost 200 years ago Friedrich Schlegel called 'socratic irony': 'a unique form of conscious dissimulation . . . It is not meant to deceive anyone . . . In it is to be included all jest, all earnest, everything transparently open and everything deeply concealed. It springs from a union of the feeling of life as an art with the scientific spirit . . . It introduces and arouses a sense of the insoluble conflict between the finite and the absolute, between the impossibility and yet the necessity of a complete communication between the two. It is the freest of all licences for through it one is enabled to rise above oneself; and yet it is the most lawful, for it is absolute necessity.'

Of this notion of Schlegel's, the wise Kierkegaard said: 'I use the expressions: irony and the ironist, but I could as easily say: Romanticism and Romanticist. Both expressions designate the same thing . . . Irony now appeared as that for which nothingness was an existent, as that which was through with everything, yet at the same time as that which had absolute power to do everything . . . In so far as irony should be so conventional as to accept a past, this past must be then of such a nature that irony can retain its freedom over it . . . It was therefore the mythical aspect of history, saga and fairy-tale which especially found grace in its eyes. With a twist of the wrist all history became myth. Poetry saga, fairy-tale-irony was free once more . . . As irony contrives to overcome historical actuality by making it hover, so irony itself has in turn become hovering' (Søren Kierkegaard, *The Concept of Irony*, 1841).

There can be few so apt summaries of the advantages and dangers of the 'New Romanticism' in contemporary painting, from the ambiguous conduct of Paula Rego's protagonist, through the equivocal status of Thérèse Oulton's landscapes between flux and solidity, the uncertain status of the human relevance of forms as props or actors in John Walker's paintings, to the elegiac note that accompanies Currie's respect for his proletarian heroes, the way in which Howson's heroic dossers teeter on the edge of losing approval as sacrificial offerings and become mere objects of pity, to the degree to which Wiszniewski's self-images are the meaningful centre or empty vessels.

Romanticism remains a shifting term, but retains its usefulness for art which is trying to work through typically Modernist ironies. These it cannot as yet abandon, even though – and precisely because – it must always remain obedient to its everlasting urge to overrun, indeed overflow, all bounds which anyone tries to set for it.

Graham Sutherland, *Thorn Tree*, 1945-6, oil

ENGLISH NEO-ROMANTICS
Malcolm Yorke

Keith Vaughan, *Dancing Figure in a Landscape*, c1942, ink, crayon and watercolour

The English Neo-Romantics looked back consciously to the spiritual values and Arcadian subject-matter in the work of Blake and Palmer. Malcolm Yorke, author of *Spirit of Place: Nine Neo-Romantic Artists and Their Times*, examines not only this relationship to Romanticism in the work of the principal artists associated with the movement but also their varied responses to the conditions of the 20th century, especially the Second World War.

'Romantic' and 'Romanticism' are the kind of slippery words you need a barrow-load of books to pin down. We can use Romantic as an art-history label to mean a roughly datable period in English cultural life (c1780-1840), or to designate characteristic subject matter (ruins, shipwrecks, mountains), or to categorise stylistic features such as the distortion of forms and heightened colour for emotional effect. If we use it in the last two ways we can discover earlier artists outside the historical period who had similar preoccupations (El Greco, Piranesi, Watteau), or later ones (Munch, Rivera, Van Gogh). Away from art discussions we might gossip about a romantic novel or a romantic proposal and mean something to do with unreality, or heightened emotion, or love. It is all blurred at the edges. In both the demotic and art contexts 'Romantic' is generally seen as the direct opposite of 'Classical', though it might be better to see them as one of many interlocking pairs which help us to make sense of the world's possibilities, such as subjective-objective, intuitional-intellectual, yin-yang, individual-collective, right brain-left brain, analogic-digital, free-ruled, night-day, organic-inorganic, and so on. We might try to symbolise the difference by placing a tree alongside a Doric column. However, no artist has ever been purely 'Romantic' or entirely 'Classical', for as Henry Moore pointed out:

> All good art has contained both Classical and Romantic elements – order and surprise, intellect and imagination, conscious and unconscious. Both sides of the artist's personality must play their part. And I think the first inception of a painting may begin from either end.[1]

On balance though, the theoretical writers on Neo-Romanticism, such as Piper, Vaughan, Ayrton, Geoffrey Grigson and Eric Newton, preferred to see all British painters of the past as heavily weighted towards Romanticism, as if this was permanently built into our native way of perceiving the world.

'Neo-Romanticism' seemed to have been first coined by Raymond Mortimer in 1942 to mark off from the Post-Impressionists, Euston Road Realists, Surrealists and Abstractionists, those artists who appealed to mystics, pantheists and those Wordsworthians who felt a 'sense sublime of something far more deeply interfused' in Nature.[2] In 1946 Robin Ironside elaborated the term to mean those who made art 'lyrical in inspiration which overcame the formal discipline of Parisian influence.'[3] He had in mind Cézanne and the Post-Impresionists as promulgated by Clive Bell and Roger Fry, and geometrical abstraction represented by the 7 & 5 Society. Ironside's anti-French attitude can be exaggerated since every Neo-Romantic painter admired Picasso, and Nash and Sutherland's works would have been impossible without the influence of Surrealism – a movement Herbert Read told them was 'the Romantic principle in art.'

The 'Neo' part of the critics label implied the modern artists' reversion to 19th-century models for their subject matter and ways of interrogating Nature for signs of spiritual values. Paul Nash, for example, was aware of Blake's work before World War I and grew up 'steeped' in Pre-Raphaelitism. His poet friend Gordon Bottomley passed on a reverence for the unfashionable works of Calvert and Palmer. When Sutherland attended Goldsmith's College in the 1920s he fell in with Paul Drury,

William Larkin and Robin Tanner, and later met F L M Griggs, all enthusiastic imitators of Palmer's luminous, but closely-textured, etchings. Piper added Turner to this list of Romantic heroes. The younger Neo-Romantics who followed them, such as Ayrton, Minton, Vaughan and Craxton, adopted the same exemplars and worked through Palmer's influence often after Nash was dead and Sutherland's vision was no longer Arcadian. Palmer's reputation was already being revived by the mid-1920s, but the steady approach of moral chaos and war in Europe must have enhanced the appeal of an artist who could see in our English landscape clear evidence of the protective hand of God, and who saw Nature as 'the veil of Heaven, through which her divine features are dimly smiling.'

The Neo-Romantics were never a conscious clique with a clubhouse and a manifesto, but their vision seemed to pervade the whole period of about 1930 to 1955 in England. Not only did they exhibit paintings which were both modern and accessible, but they earned extra money by book illustrations, book covers, posters, advertisements, ballet and theatre designs, photography, textiles, propaganda, reviewing and books on art. Their views and works appeared in influential magazines such as *Horizon*

were sent forcibly into the countryside only to find it littered with tank traps, army camps, airfields and a population supplemented by evacuee children, prisoners of war, Land Girls, GIs and Conscientious Objectors. The landscape artists were then directed back into the cities to make art from bomb devastation. If the movement had ever been nostalgically escapist it was no longer a valid accusation as the artists faced gun factories, gutted cathedrals, burned out terraces, the fire-bombed London docklands, and dumps of wrecked planes at Cowley. The abstractionists moved out of London unable, or unwilling, to compromise the purity of their art in such a public task.

Paul Nash was a war-artist twice and in *We Are Making a New World*, 1918, and *Totes Meer*, 1941, made those images which best encapsulate both conflicts for us. As a boy he had experienced dreams and waking visons of the '*genius loci*', of a 'peopled sky', vast perpendiculars, a sinister tunnel, a menacing sea, snakes, woods and 'a repeated and delicious sensation of flying'. As he grew to manhood, feeding his imagination on Rossetti and Romantic novels, he began to project his sexual longings on to softly rounded landscapes and skies across which moon-faced women trailed their hair (this was three years after

L to R: Ayrton, *Apple Trees by Moonlight*, 1945, pen, ink and wash; Sutherland, *The Garden*, 1931, etching; Nash, *The Three*, 1911, pen, ink, chalk and wash

and *New Writing* and their war-works were enormously popular in the National Gallery exhibitions organised Kenneth Clark. After the war they moved into key teaching posts in the London art colleges and so passed on their skills and outlook to new generations of artists and deigners. Novels, poetry and films of the period also seemed full of burgeoning undergrowth, moonlight and inhabited shadows. In so far as the Neo-Romantics were looking to the English countryside as an 'objective correlative' (to use T S Eliot's phrase) to channel their emotions through, then they seemed to catch a national mood. The earlier Romantics had taught us that the city was corrupt and the country health-giving; that the picturesque and Sublime could be encountered in wild mountains and waterfalls; and peace and moral insights could arrive via 'one impulse from a vernal wood'. Between the wars cycling and rambling clubs proliferated, then came the Council for the Preservation of Rural England (1926), the Youth Hostel Association (1930), Ramblers' Association (1936), the Green Belt Act (1936) and so on. This desire to get back to our 'real', rural England was fuelled by numerous guidebooks and travel posters, many of them supplied by Nash, Piper and Sutherland. Ironically, when the Blitz came people

Les Demoiselles d'Avignon had been painted). Sir William Blake Richmond (1842-1921), a son of the Richmond who was Blake's friend and fellow Ancient with Palmer at Shoreham, tried to put some reality into these works by advising, 'My boy, you should go in for Nature.' This improved Nash's drawing but he still seemed fixated on breast-like hillocks and saw three elm trees in terms of naked women. All this mooning around playing at pantheism in Metroland was finished for ever by the brutal experiences which befell him on the Ypres Salient in 1917.

Trees are upright, organic and limb-bearing and for any artist uneasy with figure drawing, as Nash was, they present obvious symbolic substitutes for people. Unlike his sensuous elms those trees on the Western front were dead and mutilated and could be used to convey the outrage he felt:

I am no longer an artist interested and cautious, I am a messenger who will bring back word from these men who are fighting to those who want the war to go on for ever. Feeble, inarticulate, will be my message, but it will have a bitter truth, and may it burn their lousy souls.[4]

Later he returned, a badly shaken war-artist without a war, to live in Dymchurch, a near-treeless landscape where the sea wall seems to present a vulnerable defence against the cold and hostile sea. Nash distrusted 'the psycho boys' who tried to interpret the unconscious archetypes which worked their way into his pictures, but he knew he was painting mind-landscapes rather than topographical records when he came to view the Dymchurch works all together.

In Romney Marsh he found a weathered log which he claimed was like a Henry Moore sculpture in the way it combined figure and landscape features. He called it *Marsh Personage* and showed it in the 1936 London *Surrealist Exhibition*, which he also helped organise. However, he and his fellow-exhibitor Sutherland shunned both the stunts and the Communist politics which the Continental Surrealists went in for. Soon Nash was searching for other logs and flints he could personalise in his pictures as Monsters, Minotaurs, Presences or Equivalents. Surrealism freed him to make unexpected chimes between a stone gate-post and the moon, or to let two disparate scenes flow into each other, such as a harbour and a bedroom. Further reading in *The Golden Bough* and Sir Thomas Browne's *Urne Buriall* gave rise to more symbols he scarcely understood himself, but which all helped him endow landscape with layers

alities and whip-like branches. In *Blasted Oak*, 1941, the bare trunk rears up in pain or rage; two oaks, one with breasts, spar in *Association of Oaks*, 1940, and several Tree Forms loom out of the green depths like sharks. Sutherland has switched now to Romanticism's other branch-line – that which leads not to health but to the macabre, evil, and Nature red in tooth and claw. He had learned the same lesson as Dylan Thomas, that Nature implacably and simultaneously creates and destroys:

The force that through the green fuse drives the flower
Drives my green age; that blasts the roots of trees
Is my destroyer.
And I am dumb to tell the crooked rose
My youth is bent by the same wintry fever.[5]

Sutherland's Pembrokeshire watercolours of the 1930s are justly famous, but they are not comfortable works with their acid colours and shadows stitched together by a rambling black line. Nor is it likely there are jovial surprises waiting round the corner in *Entrance to a Lane*, 1939, with its portcullis of brambles. He always claimed to suffer from claustrophobia but in these and later landscapes he seeks out the 'bud-like intricacy of form' and 'the womb-like enclosure',[6] and ignores the mountains which he

L to R: John Minton, *Summer Landscape*, 1945, pen and ink; Graham Sutherland, *Two Miners Drilling*, 1942, watercolour and crayon

of significance. Those images in his boyhood dreams came back to haunt him and all his ladders, steps, scaffolds, open doors and spiralling sunflowers speak of his yearning for flight into the 'peopled sky'. Ultimately, his pictures told him, it was the call of death he was painting.

Graham Sutherland, like his exact contemporary John Piper, grew up reading *The Highways and Byways* guidebooks to rural England, which were illustrated by the Palmer enthusiast F L M Griggs. After failing as an apprentice engineer Sutherland went to Goldsmith's College where in 1924 Matisse and Cézanne were thought 'inept', and Blake's *Virgil* woodcuts and Palmer's drawings and etchings were the latest craze. Sutherland, who was a new convert to Catholicism, began to etch medieval tableaux, sometimes framed by a Biblical text. In these, stars implied angels, doves the Paraclete and the laden overhanging boughs the sheltering hand of God. 'The Past for poets, the Present for Pigs' had been Palmer's motto and Sutherland's little idylls were as remote from the Depression or General Strike as Palmer's had been from the rick-burning and riots in 19th-century Kent. However, around 1929 Sutherland's mood changed, perhaps because his infant son died, and the trees began to develop nasty person-

considered boring. Soon Kenneth Clark, patron and protector of all the Neo-Romantics, summoned him to provide war pictures for the War Artists Advisory Committee; so Sutherland went to London to draw girders splintered like the roots of trees and bomb rubble like rocks on a moonlit beach. Sometimes, as in *Horned Forms*, 1944, he begins ostensibly with driftwood but the threat of the viciously armed forms is like that from a German tank. War work also took Sutherland beneath the English landscape, down the arteries of a Cornish tin-mine or into quarries where all organic life had been thrown off, like a green counterpane, to reveal the fossilised bedrock of England.

After the war Sutherland was asked to paint an 'Agony in the Garden', seemingly the perfect subject for him, but he chose instead to do a *Crucifixion*. His methods by now were literary, searching for a metaphor through which to approach his subject obliquely. Christ's agony, he found, could best be expressed through thorn branches – 'to me they were the cruelty' – and in a way the final, more literal, image of Christ's body became superfluous.

After the war travel became easier and like most English artists Sutherland went to France, eventually settling there. Now his sinister forms came out into the sunlight and glowered in front of bougainvillaea hedges. He also became a friend of Picasso, for which he was reproached by Michael Ayrton who believed Sutherland's place was in the vanguard of English art, which had found its own strength during the isolation of war and was now poised to overtake the School of Paris as the leader of European culture. It never happened, though Sutherland did return to Pembroke towards the end of his life and found, to his surprise, that he need never have left it since the roots, rocks and peculiar light were still as magical as ever. After a late flowering in these Pembroke paintings his final self-portrait shows him hunched over his sketch book almost engulfed by a wild and impenetrable thicket.

We could see Nash as the Neo-Romantics' Elder Statesman, Sutherland as its unofficial leader, and John Piper in his book *British Romantic Artists* (Collins, 1942) as their ideologist who made the Moderns' links to their ancestors explicit and respectable. 'Romantic art deals with the particular', was Piper's opening statement, meaning that by the intensity of his scrutiny of some aspect of Nature the Romantic artist can approach the universal and see the world in a grain of sand and heaven in a

asked to record charred cathedrals, the bombed House of Commons and Cardiff docks. He also recorded architectural treasures such as Windsor Castle in the expectation that the Luftwaffe would soon flatten them on their Baedecker Raids. The lowering black skies over these scenes are therefore more symbolic than literal, though King George VI's puzzled comment was, 'Very poor weather you seem to have had Mr Piper.'

After the war Piper set out to emulate those earlier Romantic artists he had written about, seeking country houses, decayed castles and village churches wherever they could be tracked down. These works gave off less moral or spiritual reverberations than Nash's and Sutherland's, being more like dramatically lit stages just before the play or opera begins. In his drawings of Snowdonia, however, I believe Piper approaches the sense of scale and feeling for foul weather that Turner had. Like Ruskin he felt the stir of muscles and tendons beneath the mountains, their 'conclusive energy, full of expression, passion and strength'. Once again a Romantic painter was tackling the Sublime.

The Fischer Fine Art exhibition of 1983 and the Barbican *Paradise Lost* show of 1987 demonstrated the wide range of artists who could conceivably be called Neo-Romantic, showing

L to R: John Piper, *In Llanberis Pass*, 1943, pen, chalk and watercolour; Michael Ayrton, *Entrance to a Wood*, 1945, oil

wild flower. He was echoing Blake and Ruskin here and deliberately contradicting Reynold's *Discourses* and Roger Fry's observation that 'the greatest art seems to concern itself most with the universal aspects of natural form, to be the least preoccupied with particulars.'[7] Piper had loved Turner's work since his boyhood. Michael Ayrton wrote a book, *British Drawings*, in the same series and took a similar chauvinistic pride in the 'characteristics of the British genius, the poetic, the satiric, the mystical, the romantic and the preoccupation with linear rhythms, which are the bones and basis of our art, and have been so for a thousand years.'[8]

Before the war Piper had put himself through a period of severe abstraction because, he said, 'I was a splashy scatterbrained painter before I took it up.' But he soon realised that what neither the abstractionists nor their Surrealist rivals 'would dream of painting is a tree standing in a field. For the tree standing in the field has practically no meaning at the moment for the painter. It is an ideal: not a reality'.[9] The Romantic had to begin from reality, even though he usually worked up the final picture in the studio. Suddenly a much grimmer reality was thrust upon Piper's attention as he was appointed a war-artist and

works by about 80 artists between them.[10] However, of the younger generation I have only space to mention four. Michael Ayrton was the Neo-Romantics' propagandist and vociferously anti-French in his reviewing – which lost him friends amongst the group. He had a Palmer period as we can see from his *Apple Trees by Moonlight*, 1945, but he soon followed Nash and Sutherland in seeing landscape as a vehicle for more disturbing moods; so in *Convulsive Landscape*, 1944, the tree forms become a copulating couple, elsewhere trees sprout breasts, and fanged skulls tower above the fields, big as cathedrals. More subtly *Entrance to a Wood*, 1945, with its bayonet-sharp branches barring a tunnel leading to sunlight must be seen as a kind of war picture.

Just before the war Ayrton had been in France with John Minton studying De Chirico, the Parisian Neo-Romantics (a group of exiled Russians – Berman, Leonide and Tchelitchew) and the French painter Bérard. These were a much more camp, theatrical group than their English namesakes and not so keen on getting their feet wet studying Nature at first-hand. Perhaps the encounter with their work delayed the development of the two young English artists rather than fostered it. Minton was enormously gifted, not so much as an innovator, but as an imitator. He quickly adopted the Neo-Romantic props of black skies, moons, ruined streets, overhanging branches, and their mixed-media graphic techniques. However he lacked both Palmer's reverence and Sutherland's pessimism and saw English landscape either as a lush Eden with young men loitering in the undergrowth as in *Surrey Landscape*, 1944, or as a mildly spooky stage set in *Dark Wood Evening*, 1945.

During the war Keith Vaughan was exiled from the London art scene to guard POWs in Yorkshire. He kept in touch through reading *Horizon* and *New Writing* which soon published his small drawings of fellow soldiers and moonlit country houses. During his leaves from service he hung on Sutherland's every word but used what he had learned to express his own private frustrations and loneliness. These feelings were fuelled by readings of Rilke, Rimbaud and Verlaine. They found outlets in such drawings as *Untitled Figure – Spring*, 1941, and *Seligkeit*, 1945, where the landscape is as expressive as the figure. Years later in his maturity, Vaughan learned how to blend the male nude back into the landscape setting so the two interpenetrated and fused.

Valley Thick With Corn, 1825, to see how spikey and aggressive the vegetation has become. The poet closes his eyes to it all. This and other drawings of dreamers, mushroom pickers, shepherds and goatherds were entirely imaginary and were, Craxton admits, an 'escape and a sort of self-protection . . . I wanted to safeguard a world of private mystery, and I was drawn to the idea of bucolic calm as a kind of refuge.'[11] Once the war was over he went to Greece and has rarely left it since, having found a refuge amongst real shepherds, goatherds and fishermen.

Other artists followed Craxton's example once travel restrictions allowed them to disperse. Picasso, Matisse and Braque reasserted their prewar fascination, and new fashions arose at home which replaced Neo-Romanticism, now associated with those shabby days of blackout and food rationing. Pop artists admired urban glitter and frivolousness, indeed all the things Romanticism warned us against. Kitchen-Sink Realists despised Romanticism's ambiguity, symbolism and lack of political commitment. The biggest blow was the invasion of Abstract Expressionism from America with its ballyhoo, giant canvases and Clement Greenberg's ludicrous claim that 'there is nothing left in nature for plastic arts to explore'. Neo-Romanticism looked

L to R: John Craxton, *Tree Root in Welsh Estuary*, 1943, oil; Paul Nash, *Eclipse of the Sunflower*, 1945, oil

John Craxton, like Minton, usually kept any private troubles out of his works, though in his dreamer and poet landscapes the tensions of war seem to have crept in. One only has to compare his *Poet in a Landscape*, 1941, with its inspiration, Palmer's

suddenly small-scale, dowdy and provincial. All these fashions, and a dozen others, have gone their way and it is perhaps time for us to look again at Neo-Romanticism's serious response to a serious need.

Notes

1 'The Sculptor Speaks', *The Listener*, 18 August 1937, p449.
2 *The New Statesman*, 28 March 1942, p208.
3 A Haskall et al, *Since 1939: Ballet, Films, Music and Painting*, London, 1948, p155.
4 'To His Wife' in *Outline: An Autobiography ...*, London, 1949, p210.
5 *Collected Poems*, 1934-52, London, 1952, p8.
6 'A Welsh Sketch Book', *Horizon*, April 1942, pp 225-35.
7 'Retrospect' in *Vision and Design*, London, 1920, 195.

8 *British Drawings*, London, 1946, p46.
9 Myfanwy Evans, ed, *The Painter's Object*, London, 1937, p123.
10 *The British Neo-Romantics 1935-1950*, Fischer Fine Art Ltd, London, and National Museum of Wales, Cardiff, July-August 1983. *A Paradise Lost: The New-Romantic Imagination in Britain 1935-1955*, Barbican Art Gallery, May-July 1987.
11 *John Craxton: Paintings and Drawings 1941-66*, Whitechapel Art Gallery, January 1967, p6.

—————— * ——————

Michael Porter, *Dovedale from the Bank*, 1987, oil

ROMANTICISM & THE MODERNIST MYTH
Keith Patrick

Hughie O'Donoghue, *Starting to Burn II*, 1985-6, oil

The 19th-century Romantic movement's break with Classicism was fundamental to the beginnings of modern art and, argues Keith Patrick, the Franco-centric view of International Modernism ignores the continuing coexistence of strong Romantic trends in the contemporary art of Spain, Germany and Britain that takes on the 19th-century inheritance and continues to bring a metaphysical approach to painting and the view of landscape.

I have the greatest respect for Robert Rosenblum's book *Modern Painting and the Northern Romantic Tradition*. Its publication in 1975 helped to establish recognition for a debate which is increasingly relevant today. And in fact I would go even further and argue that if the beginnings of modern art are to be found anywhere, they lie inextricably tangled within the roots of Romanticism and the break that movement signified with the Classical tradition.

It seems to me, however, that one of the flaws in Rosenblum's argument is in treating Romanticism as a homogeneous movement. In taking the widest possible view of the origins of the movement, Rosenblum's net draws together artists with many divergent concerns. The seemingly formidable task of reconciling the austere spirituality of Caspar David Friedrich with the political and heroic exuberance of Delacroix is left untouched by his text. Yet, while the two painters neither look nor feel to be in sympathy, both are indisputably leaders of the Romantic movement.

To resolve this paradox we must first confront one of the more fundamental elements of Western culture: that of its inherent provinciality. For many years it has not been fashionable to refute the belief that art is international, but in looking for a bridge between the origins and the contemporary reality of modern art, such a confrontation is inevitable.

Romanticism, of course, had a far broader base than a mere blueprint for a school of painting. From Wordsworth to Pushkin, and from Byron to Wagner, Romanticism embodied a new-found sense of freedom, the triumph of feeling over order, and, above all, a new perception of individualism. This spirit of the age found expression in all disciplines and the form it took was as diverse as the protagonists themselves. But, most significantly, it also took form according to nationality, evolving to the demands of each nation's culture and politics. To presuppose a greater cohesion would be a mistake and a failure to fully comprehend the provincialism lying at the heart of all European cultures. This created in Romanticism, and by implication in modern art, a number of schisms which can only truly be understood by respecting the various provincial traditions in their own right.

Inevitably, this must bring us into confrontation with the basic premise of International Modernism. Modernism asserts that, to be valid, art must conform to that free-market of formalist ideas. As Clement Greenberg put it, 'The essence of Modernism lies . . . in the use of the characteristic methods of a discipline to criticise the discipline itself. What it has abandoned in principle is the representation of the kind of space that recognisable, three-dimensional objects can inhabit.' This is clearly incompatible with the proposal that art relates to cultural patterns in the real world and in particular to the historical significance of provincial traditions.

In considering some of the major figures of this century I am frequently struck by how little they conform to this Modernist premise. The question arises, therefore, as to whether it is not just a matter of interpretation, that the Modernist view is in fact only one of a number of possible critical perspectives. As such, the Greenbergian view is valid, if soulless: the pathologist's distanced view of the impersonal body. But when this is taken to be the only perspective, to the exclusion of all others, then warning bells must sound. Still more so when confusion arises between the critical premise and the premise of the actual art object itself.

To examine the origins of this confusion, it is first necessary to look into the peculiarly dominant role played by French art. Without question, the single most significant event for the development of Romanticism was the French Revolution. The Revolution was both the fulfilment of pre-Romantic idealism and the wind on which the political and philosophical seeds of Romanticism spread throughout Europe. Although the myth was rapidly to sour, the self-evident social drama of the pre-Napoleonic years placed the events in France on centre stage. Essentially an internal affair, the struggle of the French people became the concern of liberals throughout Europe.

In this sense, the elevation of certain French artists involved in the revolutionary struggle marked the beginnings of Internationalism. But in this case the very grounds of Internationalism must be called into question, for what was taking place was nothing more than the elevation of French provincialism to international status.

Courbet and Millet venerated the dignity of ordinary life, reflecting values that foreshadowed an emotive form of socialism. Through successive generations the visual thread of French art had become fractured: what E H Gombrich refers to as the *Revolution in Permanence*. But at the same time, a die was cast that imbued French painting with that particular strand of Romanticism which was bounded by social, political and intellectual concerns.

Thus, the later progression through Impressionism and Cézanne to Cubism was increasingly one of intellectual formalism. By 1912 Gleizes and Metzinger could write 'The picture bears its pretext, the reason for its existence, within it . . . [and] can be moved with impunity from a church to a drawing room.' In other words, the artwork had become a self-defining object, without reference to the outside world. Even the superbly sensuous expressionism of Matisse was supported by concepts of involved and hermetic colour theory that would eventually lead to a near-abstraction of hard-edge forms.

It has been argued that this lineage represented a High-Romanticism, being the purest refinement of ideals of intellectual freedom stemming from the revolutionary fervour. But it

L to R: Georges Braque, *Bottle and Fishes*, c1910-12, oil; Paul Cézanne, *Mountains in Provence*, oil

We must begin with Jacques-Louis David, whose Neo-Classicism contributed to the political idealism both before and after the Revolution. In context, the Classical models of David were loaded with Romantic symbolism, a message that preached the values of freedom and equality. These ideals led not to the serenity of Classical order, but to the turmoil of bloody revolution.

Although David's Graeco-Roman Classicism ended with Delacroix, the younger artist nevertheless extended the ideals of David to their Romantic extreme. Delacroix favoured the exotic, tragic and heroic, basing his forms less on the French model of Poussin than on the masters of the Venetian School. But let us not overlook the central and didactic thread to his work, which spoke to a nation still feeling its way after the years of the Terror, and the idealism, the disillusionment and the final defeat of the Napoleonic Empire, Delacroix's message was both social and political and found a ready audience in the proliferation of liberation movements within France.

Following the Commune of 1848, yet another marked change took place in the French tradition as the exotic excesses of Delacroix gave way to a new-found realism. Artists such as

might equally be stated that the pursuit of formal order for its own sake is in fact the culmination of Classicism. Taken out of context our terms are rendered meaningless. We must therefore return to my initial point, that it is fruitless to pursue the abstract notion of Romanticism. Ultimately, we must search for the perpetuation of *specific* visual models and these we find firmly embedded within the various national traditions. In France, by the beginning of this century, only the intellectual framework bequeathed by Romanticism remained. The visual models of David and Delacroix had been eroded, but this in itself was not to be without significance for the 20th century.

The spotlight thrown upon Paris was to draw artists from all over Europe, so that the models brought into the School of Paris were truly cosmopolitan. But, if the ingredients thrown into this melting pot were international, the rules by which the game was played, the academies and various infrastructures for support and criticism, were wholly French. So it was that the precepts of French art, its standards and measures, came to dominate the beginnings of International Modernism. The cosmopolitan mix of artists only obscured the fact that in one important sense Modernism was merely a continuation of French provincialism enacted on a world stage.

When the seat of Modernism moved to New York in the 1940s, the final seal was set, for the myth of Internationalism seemed unimpeachable once enshrined on neutral soil. Inheriting the end-game of an essentially provincial European tradition, the American dealers, museums and critics were well placed to hard-sell the latest developments as a new package. The growth of the international art magazines, the fashion for luxuriously illustrated art books and catalogues whose methods of colour reproduction favoured the graphic, hard-edged and illustrative painters of the 50s and 60s, all colluded in the promotion and propagation of the Modernist myth. The importance of other provincial traditions, though real enough, became denigrated as reactionary or irrelevant, or simply overlooked.

Someday, perhaps, a comprehensive survey will be attempted from this perspective. For the moment, however, let us pursue the argument by looking briefly at some of the major figures of the provincial traditions that stood apart from the School of Paris, or, in some, cases, were seemingly operating within it.

In Spain, black humour in literature had anticipated Romanticism by over a century and its influence can be clearly felt in the

colourist, often returning to a palette that was either monochrome or sombre with earth hues. Nor was his art rooted in formal innovation, for there always remained a deep-felt commitment to his subject. One feels that the formal innovations were invariably subservient to the narrative, as if prompted by seeking the most dramatic or effectual means of expressing his theme. His expressive distortions of human anatomy evoke a clear comparison with Goya's own use of caricature, and both stray from naturalism only to make the natural world more immediate. Within the nature of that vision, the comparisons become even more striking. From the portrayal of poverty in the Blue Period, the harlequins, minstrels and acrobats of the Rose, the horrors of war expressed in *Guernica*, the anguish in the portraits of Dora Maar, the satyrs, minotaurs and mythological references of middle life, to the frank and often grotesque realisations of womanhood in the late years, Picasso followed in the footsteps laid down by Goya and the Spanish tradition.

Picasso, of course, borrowed from many earlier artists, bending composition and theme to his own ends and without regard for the integrity of the original work. It is significant, therefore, that when he reworked the *Tauromaquia* scenes of Goya, he did

L to R: Goya, *Saturn Devouring his Children*, oil; Amat, *Person Holding the Moon*; *Girl with the Head of Salome*; *Person with a Horse's Head*, all 1983, oil

early work of Goya. From the lampooning portraits of the Royal Family and the voyeurist sensuality of the Majas, to the sensitive observations of the common people, Goya's art always engaged with the reality of life. But, arguably, this was only a preparation for the later works, the so-called 'Black Paintings', which brought together an acute sense of the grotesque with an observation of social injustice and the carnage of war. Through this misanthropic perception of reality Goya interwove demons and witches from folklore, creating a twilight world of menace to mirror the times in which he lived. There is no reason to believe that Goya's motives were political in any partisan sense, but rather that his particular vision grew from a self-imposed exile. But his appeal to folk-mythology, his penetration of human nature and his undisputed skill as an artist transformed this personal vision into a universal dimension which would have lasting significance for the future development of Spanish art.

The obvious heir to Goya's legacy of Black Romanticism is Picasso. Despite his early departure from Spain and importance to the School of Paris, Picasso not only remained Spanish at heart, but, after Cubism, was also curiously removed from the developments of the Modernist tradition. Picasso was not a

so with great reverence, perhaps recognising that in Goya his own vision was already fully realised. At no other time did Picasso so overtly acknowledge this debt and there are no historical grounds for suggesting that he consciously looked back to Goya throughout his life. It is rather that the images of both artists sprang from a common soul, the origins of which lie within a Spanish tradition.

It is true that not all Spanish artists have embraced the Black tradition with such fervour. In the political isolation of the 1950s, for example, the group El Paso sought inspiration from the American abstract painters. But it is interesting to note that among the young generation there are important painters, such as Miquel Barcelo and Frederic Amat, who would clearly seem to stem from the older, indigenous tradition.

Despite the relatively late unification of Germany, its philosophy made a major contribution to Romantic thinking. Originating in the metaphysics of Kant, the way was paved for a lineage that was to include Goethe, Hegel, Schopenhauer, Nietzsche and Marx. This lineage pre-dates Romanticism, but its fundamental thinking is clearly indebted to the principles of freedom and individuality. In the visual arts, Otto Runge and Caspar David

Friedrich developed theories of landscape and nature that proposed a cosmic view of the universe. In Friedrich's own words 'The painter must not paint only what he sees in front of him, but also what he sees within himself . . .' In Friedrich we see the solitary vision of the individual proclaiming his independence and freedom. His landscapes touch upon the mystical, embracing the metaphysical and transcendent value of nature. The subject is invariably a place of seclusion, a refuge whose elements are carefully selected and ordered for their spiritual meaning. Out of this period, Germany developed a strong sense of nationhood, what Herder called *Volksgeist*. In the visual arts and in literature (notably Novalis) this coalesced into a kind of political mysticism based on the emotive bond between individual and country. The more conservative of these tendencies were certainly misappropriated by fascist ideology in the 20th century, but it should be emphasised that the central Romantic ideals of freedom and individuality could not be further removed from the reality of fascism. In considering the later developments of German art, it is possible to draw strong links between the Romanticism of Friedrich and the various forms of German Expressionism. From the pantheism of Franz Marc and the Blauer Reiter to the late

The survival of an indigenous Romantic tradition is nowhere better illustrated than in Britain. In *The Englishness of English Art* Nikolaus Pevsner observes 'England dislikes and distrusts revolution. This is a forte in political development, but a weakness in art.' The indifference of the British bourgeoisie to the French Revolution is confirmation enough of Pevsner's first assertion, but we might take exception to the latter.

By the 18th century, Britain was already well within the grip of the Industrial Revolution. This slow, relentless upheaval was in many ways no less radical than the Revolution in France, making changes fundamental to the whole nation. But the Industrial Revolution was the direct antithesis of the Romantic ideal and left British Romantics with two fundamental problems. First, the long-lived antipathy between the two nations had generated an innate distrust of all things French. Second, the difference between the two social climates saw the British Romantics fighting a rearguard stand, while their neighbours across the Channel were part of a new political vanguard. The nature of British Romantic art, therefore, assumed a radically different form, and one which was never able to reconcile itself with what was later to become the foundations of Modernism.

L to R: Thérèse Oulton, *Mortal Coil*, 1984, oil; J M W Turner, *Snow Storm: Hannibal and his Army Crossing the Alps*, exh 1812, oil

seascapes of Emil Nolde, the German Romantic lineage is thrust firmly into the 20th century. The confrontation between the so-called degenerate artists of the 20s and 30s and the prevailing political climate can only serve to emphasise the threat posed to Nazi ideology by the Romantic ideals of freedom.

In the postwar years this lineage is taken even further by artists such as Joseph Beuys and Anselm Kiefer. In Beuys we see an attempt to reconcile the personal and the universal. On the one hand there is the insistence on materials (fat and felt) with, essentially, significance only to the artist, a kind of mystical shrine to individual survival. Then again, there is the public side to Beuys, the involvement with nature through the politics of ecology. In both Beuys and Kiefer we see a complex relationship to German history and culture, the evocation of a German mythology which alternates between acceptance and denial. There is both that Romantic yearning for what is Germanic and a denial of its ultimate consequences in the 30s and 40s. Not only is the underlying concept derived from 19th-century German Romanticism, but, in Kiefer, the very model for this expression of political mysticism is drawn from the desolate spirituality of Friedrich's landscapes.

The great pre-Romantic in British art was surely William Blake. Despite fervent sympathies with the French Revolution, Blake belonged firmly to the 18th-century tradition of patriotic historicism. In both his art and poetry, Blake might be said to be singing a lament for the values eroded in the wake of the Industrial Revolution, although in reality these spiritual values had long since been eroded by the Reformation. In celebrating the myth of Albion, Blake was to look as far back as the 14th century and to the particularly English form of the illuminated manuscript figure. The elongated figures of Blake were, therefore, already resonant with the spirituality of apostles and saints and were ideally suited to the artist's vision. By implication, the metaphysical landscapes in which they were set assumed an aura of paradise on Earth, of Heaven and of Hell.

In the Shoreham period of the late 1820s, Blake's achievement was translated by one of his followers, Samuel Palmer, into the pastoral surroundings of rural Kent. Through Palmer, the sense of the spiritual came to be firmly embedded in what has since been called the British tradition of Higher Landscape Painting.

The foundations of such a tradition are, of course, also to be found in the works of Constable and Turner. What Constable described as a natural philosophy, was a detailed observation of the natural world, not for the sake of naturalism, but in pursuit of the fundamental structure of a God-made universe. Turner also believed that the Divine presence could be glimpsed through the portrayal of nature and his greatest works are invariably structured to express this power at work behind the natural world.

By the mid-19th century, Blake, Palmer, Constable and Turner, together with James Ward and John Martin, had created the beginnings of a distinct tradition in British painting. Here, the landscape, or the figure in the landscape, became the principal metaphor for a spiritual searching. This tradition can be traced as an almost unbroken line through the Pre-Raphaelites, William Morris and the Arts and Crafts Movement, Nash and Bomberg in the 1920s, the Neo-Romanticism of the 20s and 40s, the St Ives School and British abstraction of the 50s, to the artists of today.

It has often been argued that this British tradition is anti-intellectual and it is certainly true that its origins preclude that formalism for formalism's sake found in Modernism. But, as we have seen, Picasso himself did not pursue a formalist line, using innovation only as a means to more clearly re-express emotive

for a re-examination of the accepted criteria for critical evaluation. The critic Achille Bonito Oliva has tried to construct a model for national schools within a Modernist framework, but the reality is much simpler. Surely it is self-evident that the various provincial traditions, denied expression under Modernist criticism, have simply resurfaced. The formal debt owed to Modernism is clear, yet the underlying concerns remain inescapable.

If Modernist prejudices are set aside, we can see clearly within contemporary British painting the affirmation of an indigenous Romantic lineage. Earlier this year I curated two exhibitions. *The Romantic Tradition in Contemporary British Painting* (which toured to Murcia, Madrid and Birmingham) brought together works by John Bellany, Alan Davie, Christopher Le Brun, Hughie O'Donoghue, Thérèse Oulton, Michael Porter, Lance Smith, John Walker, Anthony Whishaw and Carol Wyatt. I also curated *Romantic Visions* (Camden Arts Centre, London), which presented works by a further ten younger painters, also working within this same tradition. I gratefully acknowledge the remarks of one critic who wrote that I might have included twice this number, for the fact remains that the Romantic tradition is alive and well.

L to R: John Constable, *Branch Hill Pond, Hampstead Heath*, c1825, oil; Christopher Le Brun, *Sir Bedivere*, 1983, oil

and often traditional models. Indeed, it was often the minor figures of the 20th century (such as Gleizes and Metzinger) who ultimately sought refuge in formalist rhetoric and there can be no doubt that the emphasis elsewhere has been shifted to suit the framework of Modernist criticism.

By and large, British artists of the 20th century, although rarely innovators, have accepted much of the formal developments of Modernism, but use them in the service of the older, indigenous tradition. Such hybrids are a natural consequence of the meeting of two dominant forces, of course, but does this necessarily lead to the production of good art? Too much argument of late makes the spurious relationship between tradition and worth, confusing the recognition of a tradition with an implicit value judgement of the artists themselves. While introducing a new cohesion to the first half of this century, to my mind the Romantic interpretation still reveals many of the exponents to have been mediocre artists.

The Romantic tradition would therefore appear somewhat academic, if it were not to have assumed new proportions in the present decade. The dramatic fall of Modernism in the late 70s and the equally abrupt rise of so-called Post-Modernism calls out

In the works of all these artists we see the use of landscape, or figure in the landscape, as the dominant image. The landscape is sometimes observed (as with Constable), sometimes re-structured (as with Turner), and at other times purely metaphysical (as in the model of Blake). Whatever the approach, landscape in this vein is invariably placed at the service of a spiritual questioning. It is not simply a record of time and place, nor is it fundamentally about the medium of paint itself, but questions the nature of being, the quality of life and of human values, and confronts the specific issues of conservation and ecology. The concern is often with the environment and our individual responsibility towards it.

That these are largely urban artists, choosing to paint within a landscape idiom, is wholly significant. What is Romantic landscape if not a tangible metaphor for our greater aspirations, the archetype which places man in his widest context? To Blake, Constable and Turner this ultimate context was God, the creator. In a secular age the answer is not so easily framed, with each individual approaching their relationship to the contemporary arena on their own terms. But in an age of consumerism and market forces, of ecological disaster and nuclear deterrent, are these artists of today not taking a parallel stand to their forebears

Lance Smith, *Study for the Fall of Icarus*, 1988, oil

John Bellany, *Time Will Tell*, 1985, oil

who stood against the spiritual and moral erosion of the Industrial Revolution?

Clearly such concerns cannot be the preserve of just one nation and when looking at the broad spectrum of contemporary art we see these concerns mirrored throughout the provinical traditions. At the dawn of the nuclear age, Einstein recognised that humanity had to adjust its way of thinking – on the whole, we have resolutely failed. Yet, in many contemporary artists there is an implicit awareness of such major issues. It is our great fortune that visual traditions have survived to furnish the means for their expression, visual traditions that draw upon specific models with the power to communicate that awareness to its audience. Perhaps we should consider that one of the first justifications for art is that it should be seen to be addressing the priorities of its times. Then, and only then, might we allow ourselves the luxury of formalist analysis.

The recent critical response to these ideas is some measure of the insularity of art and its observers who still remain under the dominance of Modernist thinking. Art which has become inward-looking is not equipped to face the reality in which we live.

Can we afford to respect such positions? I think not. Greenberg and his contemporary acolytes have indeed perfected the nearest approach to objective criticism, but only at the cost of dismissing all that previously constituted the soul of the work. On the mortician's slab of Modernism, the soul of the patient is unimportant. Greenbergian criticism has simply opted out of all responsibilites, save those to formalism. On the other hand, provincial and Romantic traditions not only present us with the only apparent way forward, but can quite clearly be seen to have always been a reality of art. More than that, I would argue that they are a necessity, the very life-blood that enriches and renews, and provides that essential interplay within and between cultures.

---

*

David Inshaw, *The Raven*, 1971, oil

RURALISM & THE NEW ROMANTICISM
Graham Ovenden

Graham Arnold, *A Remembered Summer*, 1985, oil

There seems to be an inherent lack of wisdom on the part of the historian/critic in his ceaseless endeavours to make absolute conclusions when forming theories as to 'isms'. Art, the more universally encompassing it be, holds many strands. Neither the Romantic nor the Classic can be entirely divorced from each other: each 'ism', however wayward, holds something of the *cantus firmus* of these two forces, thus a purity of form and sentiment (as the historian would wish)

is a fallacy, a figment of words which when dealing with a visual language finds the tenant of its vocabulary inadequate. If we assume then that Romanticism is to a greater or lesser degree an essence, and not a structural nicety to be layered on at the convenience of both artist and historian, then at least our point of departure, however fancy might fly, holds firmly within the compass of an equal temperament.

The historians tell us that English art, as with the majority of our Northern neighbours, inclines towards Romanticism or that higher level of seeing, mysticism. There is much validity in this theory, but one should not be dogmatic: one has only to consider such a landmark of Western culture as the Early English/Geometric magnificence of Salisbury Cathedral to see an austerity and purity almost unique amongst its continental contemporaries. Though, as with all such edifices, the interplay of light and shade may be called Romantic, the rigorous logic of its structure has more than a little to offer the Classicist. If in contrast we turn to the South we find those late and supreme works of Michelangelo where Classical form emerges from the marble, the image half conceived, allowing our senses to form and reconstruct. This seems to me to be an extreme example of Romantic Expressionism. I only quote both Salisbury and these masterworks of the Italian Renaissance to prove the inadequacy of a dogmatism towards a stylistic purity. Yes, English art does possess its own integrity, but here I consider Cézanne's 'little feeling' – the essence of a true sentiment – to be foremost. Style is but one note within the key structure; a chord 'harpegement' may be broken and yet still hold true to its temperament.

This short preamble is no more than to indicate the lie of a particular label when dealing with an art movement, or should I say art evolution. After all Ruralism makes no pretence towards an obsessive regard for formal niceties. Its nature is more in matter, the psychological, the paring away of art preconceptions (that 20th-century vice of innovation for innovation's sake) thus searching for what underlies the heightened reality. One has but to look at the works of Graham Arnold to see both a formidable intellect and acute visual awareness in interplay. Fragmented imagery (the Romantic heightening) is structured with great formal sensibility. It is no coincidence that Arnold possesses a profound knowledge of both literature and music and this shows not only in the sophistication of his symbolism but also in his structures. His painted collages have much in common with musical language such as fugal counterpoint. (It may be well to note that the term fugue means 'flight of the parts': within the rigours of absolute form the greatest freedom, if one wills and is able, is possible).

To a greater or lesser degree these sensibilities are shared by Arnold's fellow Ruralists. The Brotherhood, though sensitive to the 'Romantic' are in fact much closer to an older art: the Flemish *primitifs*, with their clear objective transcendentalism, seem their true forefathers. This is no mere theory as both Palmer and William Blake and the later Pre-Raphaelites found much expansion of form and sentiment in these early masters. Not least discovered was their servitude to art, a far cry from today's propaganda and hype-machine where 'masters' pose as their art, the artefacts being but a mere appendage.

One is aware that in pursuing continuity the Ruralists are out of step with the popular conception of a disposable society or culture, but then metropolitan values are but a fragment of a greater nature. The artist who is complete is more the observer than the participant in such matters. Also, with their sense of craftsmanship, the Ruralists are closer to continuity than many of our contemporary 'practitioners', who create vacuous sweeps of pigment on huge canvases, the consummation of 'if you have little or nothing to say, say it as loud or large as you can!' Indeed many Ruralist works are small in scale, Arnold and Blake in particular being masters of a modest format. But then monumentality is as much a state of mind as the physical, and the 'Romantic' essence of these small works is proven.

If there is a Romantic Ruralist theme as such, then it is a tendency towards choosing the old milestones of literary quests, something not entirely dissimilar to the PRB outlook. Here the similarity ends, for though Blake might paint a fairy, Inshaw an Ophelia, their relationship is primarily with *myth*, not the full-blooded Romanticism of the 19th century. There is more 'edge' in Ruralism than in their immediate forefathers. Nature is no less fecund but it is also fraught with the perspective of a past which in Richard Jefferies' terms is concrete, of this moment.

Perhaps the interplay of past and present is one of the most important elements of Ruralism. Both Inshaw and Arnold have voiced their philosophy on this subject. If not original it is no less precious. John Constable a century and a half before had made the definitive statement: 'I wish to give to one brief moment plucked from fleeting time a lasting and sober existence.' Or as Arnold would say, 'a heightened and ecstatic existence.' A difference of language but nonetheless a shared understanding. Certainly this moment of held time is strongly apparent in Inshaw's work. His is a deeply, one might say at times darkly, sensed Romanticism. Arnold is no less successful, but his vision is a step removed, the edge between emotion and intellect finely balanced. Blake, perhaps the most natural English artist since Spencer, has elements of both these qualities; the results can often resemble that of an icon, as much an object as a painting.

In Blake however, the founding-father of Ruralism, there are elements of a dichotomy. He is somewhat at odds with one of the most important streams of Ruralist endeavour in as much as nature is not the quintessence of his art. David Inshaw, Ann and Graham Arnold and Annie Ovenden have all produced some of their finest work when dealing with William Blake's 'vegetable nature'. Ann Arnold in particular possesses an authentic and poetic vision and not least a rich, dramatic sense of atmospheric colour.

Colour and its possible structural and emotional qualities are a Ruralist hallmark. Here we see a true quest for a rich harmonic expansion of the media. Inshaw once pointed out to me how much English painting this century had more in common with mud than pigment. When one sees the recent adulation of the incontinent school of painters (Auerbach etc) one must sadly agree; Nature is a myriad of prismatic experiences, such impoverishment of the palette can only lead to a likewise smallness of soul.

It may well be that (though no doubt the Marxist element of the art establishment would deny it) the contemporary passion for minimalist, animal emotion and all that it harbingers is closer to the individualistic self-gratification and greed of our present political masters. Both elements seem to prosper on a denial of an expansive, fruitful continuity, of true sentiment and value. Whatever the faults and failures of Ruralism it is a conscious effort to regain at least a modicum of grace. We may call its emotional response Romantic, visionary, colour expressionism, but underlying all is that first formative awareness.

Placing such a statement in words may seem too self-conscious an endeavour. This is not so, for the element of Romanticism, or if you will, wonder, in Ruralism is its natural visual vocabulary. It seems somewhat singular that this very basic part of man's interaction with his environment should prove such a critical point with the 'art gurus'. One of the supreme arrogances of 'modern' thought on art matters is its sense of small-minded, hermetically-sealed correctness of purpose. Each present novelty is the path in which art must travel, discarding previous endeavour and attainment. This is patently nonsense. Man's sensibilities and strivings remain constant, his basic humanitarian/inhumanitarian acts reenact in linear time, the sensibilities of the past are in essence our own.

It may well be that the Ruralists' self-conscious efforts to pare away our base metropolitan values, seeking, if you will, rock and earth as opposed to concrete, are a source of strength. I can well understand the sense of unease of those who practise in the insular and stifling environment of 'the art world' and all that entails when presented with an art that remains innocent of affection, an art that makes no concession to taste, an art which is both simple but nonetheless fraught. After all it is well to remind certain critics that one may escape into as well as out of an environment. No doubt if many writers on art were to remove their posteriors and walk abroad more often they might learn to see with their own eyes. I stress this point in particular because Ruralism, whatever its Romantic connotations, is not the soft underbelly of contemporary art. The opposite in fact is the case. Light plays on form, creating shadow and mystery. Ruralism is no less sensible to this disquieting interplay than it is to the prismatic ecstasy of the natural world.

Over the previous 14 years the composition of the Ruralists has undergone change. Whether Blake and Inshaw are committed as strongly to a joint exhibition programme or not is irrelevant, as their art remains as strongly personal to the original vision as ever. After all Ruralism was founded on like minds and friendship, not revolutionary principles – although it might be a type of anarchy in this day and age to be the propagandists for stern values in art. That wonderful man Chesterton made a relevant observation through the lips of his little priest Father Brown, observing that once one has ceased to believe in God one might as well believe in anything. Art has tended to take a similar path; there is no longer a point of departure for judgement. Any object, any gesture, may become art – the pile of bricks must surely contain as much substance as Albi. What nonsense!

Yes, the most humble man and his artefacts may be dignified through the means of art. No doubt a Chardin or a Cézanne could ennoble a simple building brick, allowing us to experience a greater matter through their humanity, but unfortunately the physical object remains earthbound in the most prosaic sense of the word. The essence with which Chardin may imbue the most simple object may have elements of what we call 'the Romantic', but more importantly it possesses dignity. Certainly I would wish this to be part of the Ruralist message. Blake and Arnold in particular have the ability to imbue simple objects with mystery and wonder.

Though the composition of the Ruralists may now differ from the original group of seven, the commitment of four of its founders is complete. There is also a widening circle of friends who are regularly included in exhibitions and projects. These junior members add new vitality and enthusiasm so (no doubt to the disappointment of many critics) the movement of friends continues. Whether it be Partridge's formidable work in black and white or the gentle poetry of Hewe's landscapes, there is hope yet for more telling essays on humanity and that all-encompassing relationship with the 'Great Mother'.

NEW ROMANTIC ARTISTS

by John Griffiths

Each shrub is sacred and each wood divine'. Our rediscovery of the goodness of a nature despoiled by accelerating science and technology recapitulates one of the major themes of German, French and British Romantics 200 years ago. They saw nature as a system of harmonies from which human beings had so to speak alienated themselves by trying to subjugate it to their own ideas of order. To apprehend nature proficiently, and to restore humanity to its proper place in it, the imagination had to be recharged by 'irrational' means: by the cultivation of individual wishes and sensibilities in contrast to dominative uniformity. Then, perhaps, the fissure between the conscious self and all else would close. As communal projects and relationships disappoint excessive hopes, that concern is once again our own. It is a major topic of new art. Other, related Romantic emphases also reappear: intense self-scrutiny; a new assertion of the person against the herd, and of the soul against the attributes of the body as defined by commerce; an urge to express and communicate feeling; and a greater regard for emotional, mystical, symbolic and mythic imagery. Much new figurative and some quasi-abstract painting searches the great Romantic predecessors but also the Neo-Romantics of the 1940s-50s for inspiration. Nevertheless, the new Romanticism never appears 'pure and simple'. It inherits the paradoxes of Modernism together with the modern desire for rapid and intense results; and it is often an uneasy companion of new-Classical devices which call on reason, sobriety and order to define the forms of art and of self-knowledge. Yet the same works are predominantly Romantic in hinting that a unique encounter with nature through art will afford not only aesthetic but personal harmony.

Graham Sutherland, *Welsh Landscape with Roads*, 1936, oil

NEW ROMANTIC ARTISTS

FRANCIS BACON

(1909-) Painting as the supreme source of truth about painting. The painting emerges from painting. The imagery is that of an unsatisfactory and bleak world and only the production of the work of art enables the quotidian to be transcended. This is probably the most pessimistic though nonetheless authentic version of the Romantic attitude in art.

EDWARD BURRA

(1905-1976) The exotic location as the key to painterly emotion. Louche bars, strip clubs, Marseilles night-clubs, Mexican churches, cheap market stalls, allotments, the imagery of gaudy advertising, goods and tawdry papers become a substitute nature appropriate to this part of the century. The irony is intentional but the orientation again authentically Romantic.

ROBERT COLQUHOUN

(1914-1952) The poor, the disadvantaged, and those close to animals and nature as privileged beings whose spirits only the artists can search profitably. The tramp, beggar, whistle-seller, old Irish story-teller, fortune-teller, aged solitary, ballad-singer, shepherd, cowhand, circus-folk, goat-man, actor, and so forth are presented as the ideal subject-matter for artistic truth. Old Romantic tropes resurrected in the half-light of the war and French existentialism.

JOHN CRAXTON

(1922-) The English countryside and then the Greek seascape with appropriate swains and sailors as present-day landscapes for relief from the constraint of war and later postwar austerity. Craxton has continued to offer

L to R: Robert Colquhoun, *The Lock Gate*, 1942, oil; Henry Moore, *King and Queen*, 1952-3, bronze

consistently original world of yearning and release which wears remarkably well in a new Romantic era.

DAVID JONES

(1895-1974) The perfect balance of Classical and Romantic themes sometimes precariously but always successfully maintained by a combination of personal experience through the suffering of war and spiritual assurance. Here the longing for order is one with the longing for visionary release. Myth, religion, national legend, the national countryside, and the animals and plants in it, are brought together in the human habitation so that house and natural world without are interpenetrated by the artist-poet's vision.

JOHN MINTON

(1917-1957) Palmer's England updated in war and afterwards, but also a romanticisation of the war-torn city and the working Thames. An idealisation of the working man that owed much to homosexual interests.

HENRY MOORE

(1898-1986) A successful combination of Surrealist and traditional landscape Romanticism. The texture of the natural world and natural, 'found' fragments with naturally-based shapes from various (religious) cultures as an appropriate means of releasing the yearning within for oneness with the universe.

JOHN PIPER

(1903-) Ruins, churches, and antique habitations as well worn as the English land become equally empowered means of celebrating in anticipation the union of all things visionary and gracious.

GRAHAM SUTHERLAND

(1903-1980) An expressive Romanticism by which the artist reads himself into the representation of the natural scene, which he works and embellishes with the intensity of his feeling. Colour and turning form become equal elements in this remaking of landscape.

uropean wayside shrine or worn pottery
gure, and thus placing Christ within a land-
cape or a folk tradition. This tendency itself
countered by childlike elements, such as
astel' and soft tone.

MICHAEL ANDREWS

928-) In his Highland stalking and Ayer's
ock series, Andrews removes some of the
nore nervous aspects of earlier series of analy-
es of environments. Here texture is a major
ehicle for the enunciation and discovery of
neaning. In recent works the application of
olour becomes constantly more refined and
lmost Chinese in its delicacy in order to

enhance the passages of great intensity. The
Australian series is Romantic in its implicit
reiteration of the myth of natural man supreme, but here the new emphasis on the
importance of magic as a means of self-asser-
tive identity, rather than as something important in its own right, is a new, not an old,
Romantic device.

GRAHAM ARNOLD

(1932-) Images with historical overtones are
respectfully examined and enhanced to stress
lyrical qualities. He is more of a colourist that
his equally Romantic Ruralist brethren.

ADRIAN BERG

(1929-) Richly inscribed exotic landscapes
which romanticise their underlying solidity
with a filigree touch and announce the dream
of a perfection in which inadequacies will be
repaired.

STEVEN CAMPBELL

(1963-) Supremely individualistic paintings
because they take all the artist's experience,
from philosophic reading to far too-highly
serious mentors, as very important because it
is the artist's (*A Life in Letters: Idealised*

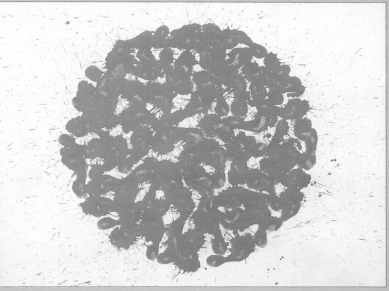

L to R: Christopher Le Brun, *Untitled*, 1983, oil; Richard Long, *Untitled*, 1987, mud on paper

ortrait of the Wig'ed Foucault). Strange
arratives are sparked off in true surrealist
ashion, but there is a constant nature to equivo-
al interrogation of the landscape tradition in
erms of other myths, such as that of the *Boy's
wn Paper* explorer.

CALUM COLVIN

961-) Stressed photographs which adum-
rate the longings of the artist and an alienated
orld which he examines passionately-dis-
assionately. The detritus of commerce, and
ven of art, are scrutinised for their authentic
alue for human relations idealised as sex,
nd to the aspirations of undeflected instinct.
1ale heroism and self-regard are celebrated
nd punctured as are several myths manufac-
red from particular male categories.

GRAHAM CROWLEY

(1950-) Figurative objects which are richly
adorned as signs of striving begin to enjoy an
almost separate life in their own right.

KEN CURRIE

(1960-) The proletarian in working and lei-
sure guises as essentially a serious type: the
apotheosis of human striving and the artist's
more worthy double. A romanticisation of the
urban working man which stands in the tradition of Masereel but also of some of the great
Christ figures of the Western tradition.

PAUL FURNEAUX

(1964-) The artist's personality and countenance explored in a multitude of mythic and
legendary guises, by recourse to folklore, and
the borrowed characters of all sorts and conditions of man and animal, but also varied
techniques of printing and production.

GWEN HARDIE

(1962-) The state of womenhood romanti-
cised by the enchancement to heroic and monumental status of simplified images of women,
or even of attenuated female bodies, but all
suffused with a soft 'feminine' light, colour
and texture which translate into the language
of painting elaborate and representative diffi-
culties about the achievements and status of
woman.

NEW ROMANTIC ARTISTS

PETER HOWSON

(1958-) The noble dosser and his avatars, the noble bruiser and so on, as heroes of the new Romantic cityscape. They are vehicles of hope and assurance. They uncompromisingly announce the residual and undying humanity of the Romantic appeal, for in the end even the landscape 'hath a human face'.

DAVID INSHAW

Rural celebrations which are also elaborate rituals of the ordered imagination, subtly interrogating the Classical groves with Romantic fancies.

CHRISTOPHER LE BRUN

(1951-) Signs of promise, recognisable Romantic images, emerge from a quasi-abstract landscape with an enlightened solidity that declares them to be more than chimeras of that imagination which here is the supreme deliverer.

RICHARD LONG

(1945-) Experiential version of the Romantic landscape tradition. The artist as priest-voyager who experiences on behalf of observer the significant patterns of land which when traversed reveal their healing truth to the visitant from an alienated world. Healing substances (mud, stone, wood) are brough from the tours to become landmarks of a new natural.

KEITH MCINTYRE

(1959-) Mainly Celtic myths interrogated for key heroic incidents and characters that rais a way of life to the same painterly status bu also act as allegorical equivalents of intensel

L to R: Michael Porter, *Constable Series*, 1986, mixed media; Thérèse Oulton, *Countenance*, 1986; Adrian Wiszniewski, *Little Bird*, 1988, oil

realised states of understanding and feeling.

GRAHAM OVENDEN

The present landscape of Britain presented in 'realistic' but enhanced moments as if perpetually sun-blessed and forever clear. No psychological states but a clarity of spirit beyond the painting, and therefore Romantic, are announced. Figure paintings recall one aspect of Romantic tradition in representing knowing innocence.

THERESE OULTON

(1953-) Highly-textured 'wild' landscapes of the emotions, painted on a grand scale which suggest possible figurative images only to subvert the meanings suggested by the intrusion of quasi-abstract forms without obvious significance. Above all a sense of mystery and openness of spirit emerges underpinned by a strange, new, unlocated sense of landscape.

MICHAEL PORTER

(1948-) Quasi-abstract landscapes with a special emotional significance for the painter. The minimal references to observable reality (for example to the Romantic traditions of the Lake District and to Constable) paradoxically enhance the pointers to mystery and light.

ADRIAN WISZNIEWSKI

(1958-) The artist and the artist's own as hero and others. The arch-Romantic search fo extension of the artist's own problems an consciousness in terms of personal and exter nal imagery, and seen as if they were univer sal. Swirling, richly whorled and inscribe structures enhance the supreme feeling tha the artist is at centre of the universe but also a vortex of personally ordained emotions.

ANDY GOLDSWORTHY

(1956-) Part of a new generation of land artist where the conceptual impetus of late-Moder art towards materials and images outside c tradition is married with a traditional concer with the colours and forms of natural object such as leaves, branches, ice, snow and feath ers in which new sculptural forms are create from natural ones.

ROMANTICALLY INCLINED
Giles Auty

Eric Ravilious, *Train Going over a Bridge at Night*, watercolour

A few years in the art business make one wary of new titles. Too often the collective names chosen to describe groups of artists are tendentious and misleading. The first rule in finding a good description is that it should be short, memorable and with positive associations. Post-Painterly Abstraction, for example, was a bit on the unwieldy side; little wonder that some of its practitioners have fallen into that chasm of oblivion reserved for

evanescent art movements which could not get their names right. Those whom others describe currently as New Romantics have got a good name, at least, in their favour. To build on this propitious start, their next need is for some form of group rationale and historical pedigree. Keith Patrick tried to supply the latter in his well-argued introductions to exhibitions staged, earlier this year, at the Ikon Gallery, Birmingham, and Camden Arts Centre in London. The problem, in my view, lay in a discrepancy I sensed between his argument and its pictorial demonstrations.

I wrote about Mr Patrick's two exhibitions, *The Romantic Tradition in Contemporary British Painting* and *Romantic Visions* in the issue of the *Spectator* dated 13.8.88. A little over a year earlier I had occasion to write, with rather more enthusiasm, about *A Paradise Lost: The Neo-Romantic Imagination in Britain 1935-55*. A number of writers, of whom I was one, commented unfavourably on the exclusion of the Neo-Romantics collectively from the major survey show, *British Art in the 20th Century*, staged in January 1987 at the Royal Academy. A subtle shifting of critical ground seems to have taken place since then; British Romanticism, old or new, is being proposed increasingly as a hitherto unrecognised alternative to some of the inherent shortcomings of Modernist thought – and thus as a guiding beacon for contemporary artists in the present dark night. Peter Fuller's latest book, *Theoria: Art and the Absence of Grace,* argues against barren, formalist orthodoxy and on behalf of an older, Romantic and spiritual tradition personified already in the writings of Ruskin.

All in all, the role of the New Romantic seems to be gaining increasing critical credibility. However, this does not prevent the more cautious among us questioning the right of certain artists to assume this role. We may all call ourselves anything we choose but if language is to have any stable and agreed meaning then titles need justification. Of course, the term Romantic, as applied to art, has always held different shades of meaning, even for the educated. Now, as in the past, opinions differ as to which artists should or should not be included under the Romantic banner. In *Modern Painting and the Northern Romantic Tradition* Robert Rosenblum presents a cogent speculation which tries to redefine the boundaries of Romanticism and makes less than obvious links between artists as disparate as Caspar David Friedrich and Mark Rothko. The linking threads that Mr Rosenblum suggests tend to be spiritual rather than formal. Some may feel reservations about his findings. In the end, the best we can do is opt for the theory which endorses our own discoveries most closely. Where we cannot find this ready-made, we are obliged to construct some alternative of our own.

Robert Rosemblum proposes his historical connections through the recurrence of certain kinds of Romantic vision: the apocalyptic, the transcendental, the mystical, the pastoral. Where a type of vision reappears in different eras this is sufficient, in his view, to argue a historical continuity. My reservation about this is that similarities in vision do not presuppose similarities in artistic ability to express them. I am prepared to believe that any number of visual artists may possess visions of majestic complexity. However, unless I learn about these visions through

J M W Turner, *Rocky Bay with Figures*, oil

other means – via an alternative outlet such as poetry, for instance – I can judge them for myself only through the visual evidence. Art-historical theories which rely heavily on artists' thoughts, rather than on their visual execution, discount the danger of what I can best describe as formal inadequacy. The chosen vehicle must be capable of sustaining the weight of the artistic vision.

The history of Modernism centres not just on the embrace of the new but on the rejection of the old; indeed we might gauge how 'modern' something is largely by the degree of its schism with former practice. This century has seen the invention of a number of art forms which by their nature are incapable of bearing the weight of any major humanitarian or mystical vision. Generally they were not meant to. Do you ever wonder whether Goya could have worked with equal success through geometrical abstraction, say, or Minimalism? Could Constable and Delacroix have made equally lasting impact through the media of Pop Art or Performance? These are not questions which many artists or historians care to ask themselves, preferring to see the history of visual art as one ruled by temporal stylistic imperatives. To this day, many continue to believe that artists are compelled to work

in this or that way in any particular era. I do not believe in this notion nor in that of *Zeitgeist* which often signifies little more today than an ability to obtain and read art magazines. Observers may note that in Russia, where up-to-date Western art publications are hard to come by, simultaneous and supposedly spontaneous outbursts of stylistic spirit seldom seem to occur.

You may or may not agree with my proposition that a number of modern formal means would have proved inadequate for the purposes of Romantic artist of the calibre of Blake or Géricault. On the other hand it would be hard to deny that many who have used such means in this century have benefited by the places they claimed for themselves in the history of modern art. Avant-gardism was not without practical and pecuniary benefits for those in its van. Whatever artists may have lost through the abandonment of truly expressive language they have been compensated for, in a worldly sense, by their enthusiastic reception into Modernism's halls of fame. Mark Rothko, whom Robert Rosenblum proposes as a late-blooming exemplar of the Northern Romantic tradition, might be thought such an artist. In a perceptive essay written for the catalogue of the major exhibition of Rothko at the Tate Gallery in 1987, Irving Sandler wrote:

John Constable, *Salisbury Cathedral from the Bishop's Grounds*, 1823, oil

'Were Rothko's paintings of transcendental experience too private, too humanly vulnerable, too reduced, even impoverished in their pictorial means to be major?' By eliminating line and relying entirely on soft, amorphous forms to do his latter artistic bidding, Rothko placed great and possibly unbearable strain on colour. Indeed colour became his sole vehicle for distinguishing different forms of content.

Turner did not make this mistake. In later life he may have seemed to generalise more in his art but I feel it is only hard-line Modernists who suggest now that the late works were the summit of Turner's achievement. Not long ago a school of criticism existed which made artists such as Turner and Whistler the formal forerunners of Abstract Expressionism and colour-field painting. Similarly erroneous theories were advanced also for Cézanne. Lionello Venturi refuted these in his critical study of 1936: 'It would be the gravest of errors to see in Cézanne a precursor of all the tendencies of painting that came after him: as it were, a seed from which a whole forest has grown.'

Apologists have made liberal use of the names of Turner, Whistler and Cézanne in formulating those backward constructs of history through which they hope to provide modern artists with the blood-lines of historical pedigree. I do not suggest that my fellow contributors Robert Rosenblum and Keith Patrick indulge in this sport, but wish simply to point out its dangers. Those seeking to construct historical justifications today face a special problem because Modernism is characterised most clearly by its schism with past practice. (Where such an abrupt break does not take place we are dealing with some degree, at least, of continuation of tradition.) Modernism drew credit from its severance with tradition. Indeed, its language is full of examples of the heady rhetoric of radicalism, revolution and divorce – one need look no further than the Futurist Manifesto of 1910. In short, Modernism did not simply bend the spine of art; it broke it deliberately. Unfortunately for those seeking historical authentication for present actions, it is across this gaping chasm of detachment that they must try to lay their lines. Until recently, the artistic attitude of our era was founded in an assumption of progress in art analogous to that found in technological evolution. Although we acknowledge our forebears, we tend to do so dismissively on the assumption that we have grown steadily in enlightenment. These are comforting assumptions, but ones on which the demise of Modernism casts a threatening shadow.

John Walker, *Labyrinth I*, 1979, oil

The artists chosen for Keith Patrick's *The Romantic Tradition in Contemporary British Painting*, first shown in Murcia and Madrid and latterly in Birmingham, were John Bellany, Alan Davie, Christopher Le Brun, Hughie O'Donoghue, Thérèse Oulton, Michael Porter, Lance Smith, John Walker, Anthony Whishaw and Carol Wyatt. The first two apart, the remainder may strike many as artistic hybrids. I am sure the works of every one of the latter eight would have been accepted, without fuss, for almost any Abstract Expressionist exhibition staged during the 60s. Alan Davie, of course, really was included in such exhibitions but remains an artist who deals primarily in the potency of symbols. One of the last classifications under which I would expect to find him would be that of Romantic. Indeed, his friend and former gliding partner, the late Peter Lanyon, was probably closer in his art to Romantic principles. John Bellany, for his part, showed the early influence of Beckmann but moved on to create his own vocabulary of metaphysical symbols. The remaining artists in Mr Patrick's show deal largely in formal ambiguities and loosely expressionistic handling. Often faint Romantic allusions to natural phenomena can be detected in their paintings: sea, sky, skulls, barren heaths, the odd whirlpool etc. The

inclusion of such vague and often semi-veiled allusions might have been looked on as daring during the heyday of Greenbergian formalism, but seems merely cautious today in an age of supposed artistic pluralism. The vaguer the pictorial concoction, the greater the hedging of artistic bets; this is what I mean when I describe most of these artists as hybrids. The works of all eight remain recognisably 'modern' paintings, full of surface felicities and answerable still to the formalist canons of two-dimensional design. Most of this work represents at best only a cosmetic Romanticism, formulaic, unfocused and seldom more than skin deep. It may offend few but will satisfy fewer. My guess is that its real origins lie, in the main, in the Modernist hegemony which prevailed in art education from the mid-50s and which has continued, in a less altered state than many people imagine, to the present time. I fear that much of what students learnt was simply how to produce art that was acceptable to their tutors or, later on, to awards panels and those in the commercial gallery and museum hierarchies. The importance given to purely formal relationships was high on the list of known requirements. In short, young artists became trapped into meeting the stylistic criteria of others, often without realising this was happening, and

Peter Lanyon, *Porthleven*, oil

Thérèse Oulton, *In Fidelity*, 1987, oil

at great cost to their own expressive needs. Mr Patrick admits the existence of such pressures but is wrong sometimes in his chronology: 'The crisis provided by the demise of a Modernist tradition in the 60s and 70s was also a liberation, giving sanction to a dramatic widening of horizons'. In fact, Modernist influence had not begun to decline by the 60s – nor is it dead today, by any means. A majority of those now occupying top positions in the Western museum hierarchies trained under the rigid orthodoxies of Modernism and absorbed these as second nature. With the possible exception of John Bellany, not one of Keith Patrick's selected artists either challenges or suggests an alternative to such orthodoxy. Indeed, the confusion of aims of most of these artists is reflected tellingly in their catalogue statements. Mr Patrick remains correct in his belief that Britain has a long and worthy tradition in Romantic art, and one which is still relevant. He argues his case well but illustrates it less convincingly. On the evidence of the two exhibitions he has staged so far, New Romanticism fails to offer a new or credible identity. But was the earlier, Neo-Romantic movement, which flourished in Britain before, during and shortly after the last war, any more of a success? To what extent did it revitalise and carry forward a

major British tradition?

One of the first books on art I read as a small boy was John Piper's *British Romantic Artists*. I know its illustrations by heart and still retain my original copy, published in 1942. The first paragraph of the book has a certain relevance to the subject at issue: 'Romantic art deals with the particular. The particularisation of Bewick about a bird's wing, of Turner about a waterfall or a hill town, or of Rosetti about Elizabeth Siddall, is a result of a vision that can see in these things something significant beyond ordinary significance: something that for a moment seems to contain the whole world; and, when the moment is past, carries over some comment on life or experience besides the comment on appearances.'

The present is a good time to recognise the extent to which 20th-century formalism has impoverished our pictorial vocabularies, for no-one truly sees the world solely in terms of relationships between colours and forms. New-born babies tend to look 'formally' similar but naturally the mother in the maternity wing does not want just any baby, she wants the particular one which happens to be her own. The Neo-Romantics made much of the tradition of the particular, a point affirmed by

Hughie O'Donoghue, *Red Earth III*, 1985, oil

the title chosen by Malcolm Yorke for his recent book about them *A Spirit of Place*. The problem of the particular is that it cannot be dealt with satisfactorily in art merely through vague, formal generalities. Artists dealing with the particular need to understand the perceptual world in all its visual complexity and subtlety. There is no doubt that the Neo-Romantics were aided in such a quest by the older, more traditional form of art education most of them underwent. Visual literacy demands knowledge and understanding of the seen, reinforced by drawing ability. In art, as in literature, the expansive sweep becomes more convincing from hands which can also get the details right.

Neo-Romanticism was the last largely linear movement in British art and also the last with strong rural links. Most of its practitioners lived or worked in the country for some period of their lives; indeed, the pastoral vision was at the heart of this renewal of the Romantic tradition. Before the last war, the country idyll represented a Romantic ideal to a far greater extent than it does today. Many people took pride in their knowledge of flora, fauna and country ways. A number of artists not generally considered part of the Neo-Romantic movement nevertheless summed up the element of rural mysticism as quintessentially as

any of the central band of practitioners; Frances Hodgkins and Eric Ravilious especially. Much of the best Neo-Romantic work is on paper, often on a modest scale. Although the same could be said of work by Palmer from the Shoreham period and by Blake, it has become the modern critical custom nevertheless to associate modest size with modest achievement where more recent art is concerned. The modern, purpose-designed museum contributes to this since it requires work of giant size to fill its inflated architectural proportions.

In 30 years of looking at art and speaking regularly with painters, the greatest change I have noticed has been a gradual decline of artistic idealism. Nearly all the artists I met in my youth expressed themselves and behaved as artistic idealists. Cynicism and disillusionment are more the norm today, perhaps because the opportunities for wealth and easily earned fame are so much greater. For the Romantic vision to survive and flourish in a worthwhile form in Britain, we require first a radical reappraisal of our art-education system to encourage the rebirth of visual literacy. Yet this is only half the battle. The even greater problem lies with the non-idealistic nature of the modern artistic mind. Without genuine idealism, Romanticism is dead.

Hermann Albert, *Two Women by the Spring*, 1987, oil

MODERN MYTHS
Hugh Cumming

Kathryn Freeman, *Allegory of Imagination, Vision of the White Horse, oil*

The 1980s have witnessed the emergence of a new generation of artists who draw on tradition in a variety of ways. Artists such as Mariani, McKenna, Andrejevic and Albert all reveal a distinct yet profound appreciation of the Classical tradition. In the work of these artists Classical elements often merge with Romantic concerns as part of an eclectic aesthetic which is examined here in the light of a significant recent exhibition at the Boise Gallery, Idaho.

The emergence of what has been described as a Classical renewal in contemporary art is not as mysterious as it first appears. In fact the exact nature of this renewal or resurgence hides what is sometimes an eclectic combination of stylistic devices and themes as well as a diverse range of intentions. What is clear is that both artists and critics are seeking new critical and theoretical means of describing what has in the 80s been an extensive shift in the nature of contemporary art. This has manifested itself in the art press and exhibition circuit as a series of well-publicised potential movements from the Zeitgeist that heralded in this decade to the New Classicism and Romanticism that herald in the next. The climate of the decade has been one in which a loss of an at times evangelical faith in the claims of conceptual and abstract art has given way to a greater openness to traditional styles, themes and subject matter. What appeared to be an enormous historical chasm between the past and present has given way to an often startling resurrection of tradition. In fact history and tradition have even been described by two leading contemporary Classical artists as part of a contemporary avant-garde art. Both Carlo Maria Mariani and David Ligare have cited the spirit of Duchamp in their use of Classical composition and subject matter. However the novelty of such gestures has now given way to a more serious and sustained body of work that has been rapidly consumed as part of a new critical impetus that advocates the stylistic order of Classical composition and the subject matter and theme of Classical painting as an integral part of current art.

The work of artists such as Carlo Maria Mariani, David Ligare, Hermann Albert and Ian Hamilton Finlay has in fact more than anything else provoked a climate in which given notions as to what is acceptable and possible in contemporary art has changed. The choice of certain subject matter and a highly ordered representational style initially provoked the use of the term Classical in describing what is a significant phenomenon. This in turn has led to a whole gamut of traditional categories being resurrected in order to describe what is happening. The current debate has now reached the stage of development where the efficacy of those terms is brought into question, not only because the works of art defy the limitations of easy categorisation, but because they incorporate elements within their aesthetic which are contemporary and novel. Part of the essential argument behind much of the new Classical painting is the notion that history and tradition are eternally relevant and, therefore, to say that tradition is not contemporary is fallacious as by its very nature it is always pertinent. 'The ideology is Classical and I believe that it comes to the forefront in every century in different ways. In addition to that I see my work as the swan-song, the last expression of the concept of beauty and the sublime'. Mariani's description of the nature of Classicism in his work echoes the sentiment that the Classical spirit has a cyclical presence in culture. However Mariani's description of his work is coloured by a kind of apocalyptic Romanticism that comes from his awareness of the state of contemporary society. He is also aware of the cultural undercurrent of which his work is a part: 'It is a desire in the unconscious of the world today, a world characterised by fame and greed, for the transcendental in beauty.' Yet at

Above: Milet Andrejevic, *Apollo and Daphne*, 1969, oil; *Below:* David Ligare, *Landscape for Bauchis and Philemon*, 1985, oil

Above: Bruno Civitico, *Diana and Acteon*, 1983, oil; *Below:* Stephen McKenna, *Jupiter and Antiope*, 1983, oil

Gérard Garouste, *The Commander and the Pink House*, 1985

the same time he describes his work as the 'swan-song, the last expression of beauty and the sublime'. It is this awareness that gives Mariani's haunting figures their edge. They are neither reconstructions nor pastiches of previous models but contemporary embodiments of an ideal that is tempered by an awareness of its finality. Despite such a *fin-de-siècle* sentiment one could almost describe his view of history as atemporal. It would be tempting to describe it as essentially modern in that history and tradition are seen as a series of poetic fragments that are just as valid today as when they originally appeared. The idea that there is a grand linear progression of form and style in the history of culture is one that he seems to reject. What he seems to acknowledge is that an artist is free to paint and assert what he wants in spite of the orthodoxy of the age.

What has characterised part of the critical attitude towards the reassertion of tradition in contemporary painting are the claims of a Post-Modern aesthetic. That is that the Classicism of Mariani, Ligare and McKenna is seen as part of the same cycle of the revival of historical styles the Neo-Geo of Philip Taaffe or the Neo-Expressionism of Baselitz and Lüpertz. Yet the use of Post-Modernism as an all-embracing concept for the culture of

the present easily masks many contradictions and complexities. To call an interest in tradition and history Post-Modern because it is contemporary, is in a sense fallacious. This is because it ignores the fact that history is and has been continually present as an influence even at the very point that it was rejected. It also ignores the fact that many techniques, themes and subjects which would now be called traditional, have in fact been influential even when they were supposed to have been rejected and superseded.

Another characteristic of the Post-Modern critique is its advocacy of eclecticism, that is that for a work of art to be Post-Modern it should combine or marry traditional style and theme with something that is contemporary. This however has been an essential aspect of any art apart from the pastiche or copy which given a length of time is seen to recall by means of its very nature the age or era in which it was created. Claims of an ironic use of traditional style or theme again are not consistent with the intentions or practice of many of the artists who can now be called Classical. For example it would be difficult to discern the irony in the work of David Ligare who seems to be an artist who is utterly earnest in his desire to create a Classical ideal for today through his combination of mythical subject, landscape and figure. In fact what would seem to characterise much of new Classical art is the almost pure conviction that a Classical style and theme is not only possible but pertinent. The work of artists such as David Ligare and other Americans such as Bruno Civitico, Edward Schmidt, James Lecky and Elsie Russell Harrington reveal a total lack of inhibition about their theme or style, and in fact one is hardly aware of a sense of impossibility or inappropriateness associated with their advocacy of Classical scene and theme. What one has in effect is a series of diverse attitudes towards tradition and the Classical past.

Stephen McKenna, for example, would seem to have a very different attitude towards tradition. In his paintings of Pompeii he is attracted by the composite image of architecture, wall paintings and nature, rather than recreating an image of the past, either historically or aesthetically, or creating an ideal. What really appeals to him is the nature of such a place as Pompeii after the passage of time. McKenna is sensitive to the forms, shapes and images of the period but not as they originally must have appeared. What we see in his paintings is the strange silent presence of ancient culture after years of decay and the onslaught of natural growth. McKenna reveals a profound fascination with Classical art yet at the same time he is aware of the cultural gulf created by the passage of time and the changes in the nature of culture. What McKenna reflects in a way is the contemporary condition of commenting on a culture with which society is no longer profoundly conversant.

Despite the difference between an artist such as McKenna and many current American artists the coherence of Classicism in contemporary art has become increasingly publicised. Many artists who are essentially distinct and who have nothing more in common than that they have an interest in Classicism are increasingly grouped together. Yet despite the differences it is undeniable that Classicism in a variety of forms and guises is becoming an important part of contemporary art. One of several influential exhibitions to recently acknowledge this was *Modern Myths: Classical Renewal,* a travelling exhibition curated by Sandy Harthorn at the Boise Gallery of Art in Idaho. The exhibition brings together leading European and American Classical artists and is significant in acknowledging the shared themes and interests that inform their work, giving what amounts to a powerful representative picture of the diverse strengths of these artists. The exhibition's main thesis is 'the importance of retaining a standard pictorial language'. It chooses to emphasise mythological and allegorical subject matter as the means of illustrating this. Myth and allegory are seen as a kind of eternal cultural link that has a role beyond the aesthetic one. 'Allegories, closely related to myths, are symbolic stories whose characters are the embodiment of moral qualities. Both devices provide arresting details of heroes and divinities which are designed to reveal serious messages of social, political, religious and philosophical significance.' What is seen to be significant in new Classical art is that it relates to a recognised traditional pictorial idiom, that it shows an awareness of the fact that there is a relation between the contemporary and traditional and that moral and social themes are reflected.

Despite the overall coherent thesis of the exhibition there are divergent styles and themes within the works of the individual artists. Perhaps the nearest to a coherent group is that of New York artists 'who had made the decision to "go back to figuration"' when American post-war Modernism was at its height. These are seen to include Alfred Russell, Gabriel Laderman, Lennart Anderson and Milet Andrejevic 'who sought to utilise rendering and to reintroduce representational drawing particularly anatomy, precisely because the standards of beauty are based on the human figure'. Of the artists mentioned the exhibition features works by Milet Andrejevic who specialises in contemporary realisations of Classical scenes, such as *Apollo and Daphne* where a Classical myth is set in contemporary America. Andrejevic however does not seek to clothe the traditional story in a fully contemporary setting. His paintings combine emblems of the present such as distant skyscrapers and contemporary dress with Classical perspective, an unpolluted rural vista and carefully arranged figures. Then there are artists such as Elsie Russell Harrington whose *Bacchanale* seeks to create an atemporal world that is neither contemporary nor ancient. On the other hand artists such as James Lecky and Edward Schmidt echo the figures and groupings of many traditional artists yet make no attempt to relate them to the objects and clothes of today. In fact they seem to accept as a matter of course that there is no need to force relevance because it is understood that their theme and world is in itself relevant.

Many of the paintings by American Classicists marry a strong awareness of tradition with a powerful realist sensibility. This is revealed either in the need of some artists to combine contemporary clothes and objects or in the photorealist understanding of figure and background. Jon Swihart's picture of travellers discovering a wayside shrine is perhaps the best example of this strange marrying of American realism and more traditional poses and themes. In fact underlying the thesis of this exhibition is the realisation that behind much of the new Classical art is a desire for a representational art that is strongly thematic. Other artists such as John Nava do not however fit easily into this thesis. Nava does not seem interested in myth or traditional representation in the same way as Andrejevic is. His pictures are commentaries on the nature of form and relate human to architectural and natural to artistic form by means of a kind of collage of images rather than traditional one-point perspective. An artist such as Kathryn Freeman is closer to Stanley Spencer in her realisation of a contemporary allegory, and the European artists Gérard Garouste and Hermann Albert are respectively more baroque and poetic than the clear and meticulous David Ligare.

What this exhibition reveals is the variety of styles and influences at play within what is nominally called the New Classicism. In fact it is possible to see the ahistorical assertiveness of many of the artists concerned almost as a Romantic gesture, that their belief in harmonic relations is a Romantic gesture in defiance of the dominant modes and spirit of the age. The notion that art should be relevant to an age through the replication of its surface reality is a fallacious one and no longer fashionable yet it often lies behind the reaction to the work of artists who are concerned with contemporary Classicism. In a way, what many of these artists suggest is that tradition is continually relevant purely by means of its use. Futhermore the work of many of the artists here reveals that in some instances a strict understanding of what Classicism is will not suffice in attempting to understand their work and in others that a profound respect for Classical tradition can produce powerful contemporary work.

———————— * ————————

Mimmo Paladino, *A Surrounded Figure*, 1983, bronze

ROMANTIC SCULPTURE
Mary Rose Beaumont

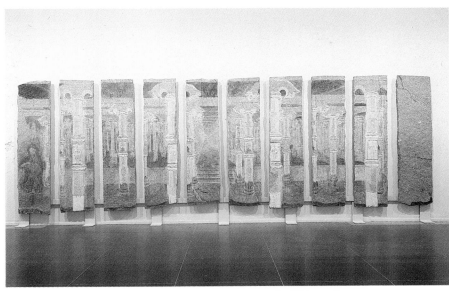

Stephen Cox, *Thousand Pillared Hall*, 1986, granite

Contemporary Romantic sculpture draws not only on landscape and nature, but contains strong elements of metaphor and allegory taken from many cultures – from the familiar images of Mediterranean mythology to Hindu iconography, Chinese tomb sculpture and Egyptian wall painting. Mary Rose Beaumont here surveys recent international sculpture and points up common Romantic threads in a body of work that is richly diverse.

In his essay 'British Romantic Artists' included in *Aspects of British Art*, published by Collins in 1947, John Piper wrote: 'Romantic art . . . is the result of a vision that can see in things something significant beyond ordinary significance: something, that for a moment seems to contain the whole world; and, when the moment is past, carries over some comment on life or experience besides the comment on appearances.'

In the same year Geoffrey Grigson wrote: 'Romantic artists of all countries share a tendency to be emotional and unintellectual about their art, to mix their art intimately with their religion, which was often of a personal, unorthodox, mystical kind.' Piper's statement still holds true 40 years later, but Grigson's seems hopelessly dated – stuck, like a fly in amber, in the era of Neo-Romanticism of which he was a leading exponent. Artists are not, with the possible exception of the naive or 'outsiders', unintellectual, and the word passionate would be an improvement on emotional. Religion seems to be now, as then, out of place, although personal, unorthodox and mystical are still valid.

Many of Stephen Cox's sculptures have Classical associations, particularly those he made when he was working in Italy. He has now been in India since 1985 and his recent pieces show a strong identification with the materials and forms of Indian art and architecture. He works, in collaboration with local craftsmen, at the Government College of Architecture and Sculpture, Mahabalipuram, near Madras, using granite, the local material. A sculpture of extraordinarily compelling beauty is *Thousand Pillared Hall*, 1986, made of separate slabs of granite stained with an image of the vast chamber in rust and copper sulphate.

The remarkable perspectival effect draws the viewer into illusory space. More overtly Romantic is *The Brides of Manamia*, 1986, in granite, silk and mixed media, which convincingly recreates an Indian marriage ceremony. Besides granite sculptures inspired by Indian temple sculpture, Cox this year has cast in bronze figures drawn from the gods of Hindu iconography, pairing, for example, Ganesha, the elephant-god, with Devi, the mother goddess. Headless, armless, and amputated at the knees, they are indirect derivations of their prototypes. The clue to Ganesha's identity is his penis which takes the form of an elephant's trunk.

Mario Rossi also adheres to a Classical canon in both his paintings and sculptures, often using a Classical image, such as that of Louis XIV in the guise of a Roman general, and then pointing up its Romantic associations by placing its height against a stormy sky. In his bronze sculpture *Phenomenon 1870*, 1986, he sets a deliquescent Ionic column atop a tangle of branches, so that it resembles an uprooted tree, symbolising perhaps the power of Nature over man-made forms. The sculpture refers to a visit Victor Hugo made in 1870 to Guernsey, where he planted a tree, as a believer might place a candle in a church, in the hope that it would grant his desire for a United States of Europe. As this was at the beginning of the Franco-Prussian war, which proved disastrous for the French, it seemed a forlorn hope indeed.

Victor Hugo, besides being an artist himself, was often portrayed by other artists, most notably by Rodin, who made several versions of a memorial to the great man, although these are not among his more successful works. Rodin also made an enormous number of studies of Balzac's head and nude body as well as an immense statue of the writer which is perhaps one of the greatest and most Romantic memorial sculptures ever made, perpetuating him as gargantuan in more senses than one. Predictably it was rejected by the Société des Gens de Lettres, the commissioning body: not until 1936 was it cast in bronze and finally, in 1939, installed at the crossroads of the boulevards Montparnasse and Raspael. In the *In Tandem* exhibition at the Whitechapel in 1986 Julian Schnabel showed an inert monolith which he had the temerity to entitle *Balzac*. Made in 1983, it is clearly indebted to Rodin but has failed entirely to catch the bravura of that masterpiece, let alone the skill and devotion which went towards its formation. Schnabel's *Balzac* is a totemic image idly cobbled together, unredeemed by the twig sprouting from its head, which appears to imitate a thought-bubble in a strip cartoon.

A crossing of boundaries is achieved by Barry Flanagan in his sculptures based on the horses of St Mark's in Venice. The horses have a Classical pedigree – they date from the Graeco-Roman period – but their position on the facade of the Byzantine

core of his work. In Madras in 1983, with the help of local artisans, he created a whole battalion of little figures, each 68 cms high, in papier-mâché and clay. Each figure is identical and – a surreal touch – they are the same from both sides. They have the appearance of having just been resurrected from an earthy grave and seem, in John Piper's words, 'to carry over some comment on life or experience besides the comment on appearances'.

Mimmo Paladino was also born in the south of Italy, near Benevento and his works carry within them a sense of an indefinable antiquity, of prehistoric rites and rituals whose meaning we can only guess at. *A Surrounded Figure*, 1983, combines references to Chinese tomb sculpture with suggestions of Egyptian wall painting, particularly in the Anubis-like creature which leers fawningly up at the seated figure. Evil is disturbingly present. In 1984 Paladino made a huge bronze portal entitled *South*, which was exhibited outside the Italian Pavilion at the 1988 Venice Biennale. Covered with human and animal figures, rods, poles and a conflagration, it would seem to be Paladino's Modernist version of Rodin's *Gates of Hell*.

German artists have always been drawn to Mediterranean culture, and therefore inevitably to Italy, but they have tended to

L to R: Markus Lüpertz, *The Burghers of Florence*, 1983, bronze; Shigeo Toya, *Range of Mountains*, 1985, wood

basilica of St Mark's is highly Romantic. Flanagan has taken advantage of this duality and subverted the image for his own purposes. In *Horse and Cougar*, 1984, the horse carries his unlikely jockey with a dignified insouciance. We are conditioned by Stubbs' painting of a lion attacking a horse to expect a deathly conflict, but Flanagan confounds our expectations by making his image take on the nature of a fairground outing.

Francesco Clemente was born in Naples and, although he now divides his time between Rome, New York and Madras, he retains the spiritual link with the past which is inherent in Italians from the South. On the one hand there is the inescapable presence of Pompeii and Herculaneum, a constant reminder of a past civilisation, and on the other there are the churches with their dark interiors and paintings of saints and martyrs. Caravaggio spent some time in Naples when he was forced to flee from Rome after killing a man in a brawl and painted the great altarpiece in the Church of the Pio Monte della Misericordia showing *The Seven Acts of Mercy*. Clemente stirs into his folk memory of pre-Christian art and Neapolitan Renaissance art a knowledge of Hindu iconography and an interest in metaphysical systems. It is the human body, usually his own, which forms the

take from it the Romantic and mythological, rather than the Classical, aspects of its earlier civilisations. Markus Lüpertz has lived and worked in Milan, from where he could look eastwards to Greece, and the riches of her cultural past, and westwards to France, where once again the figure of Rodin must be invoked as the begetter of new possibilities for 20th-century sculpture. Lüpertz's *Shepherd*, 1986, draws on the Classical prototype of the 6th-century BC Attic sculpture, *The Calf Bearer*, in the Acropolis Museum in Athens, but he has interpreted it in a rough, deliberately anti-Classical manner more in tune with Picasso's *Man with a Lamb*, 1943. The meaning of Lüpertz's sculpture is ambiguous: is the lamb being brought to the slaughter, as the calf was in the Attic sculpture, or is it being protected from harm, as is Picasso's? The challenge of Rodin's *Burghers of Calais* inspired Lüpertz to make a series of *Burghers of Florence* in 1983, painted bronze heads, at once coarse and humorous, ranging from the Prince to a gaping tourist. Lüpertz is a ruthless appropriator, but the images he re-presents are incontrovertibly his own.

Landscape and natural forms have played a large part in the sculpture of the 1980s, perhaps because of the increased interest in the environment and knowledge of the perilous state of the world's resources. Landscape has been regarded as Romantic subject-matter in Britain since the 19th century, and the legacy of Constable and Turner is still potent. The chief protagonist of the romance of Nature is Richard Long, who takes extended walks through remote areas, where at some point he rearranges a few stones or builds a cairn, photographs them and moves on, leaving them to the ravages of wind and weather. The only record is the photograph. Long's more tangible sculptures take the form of lines or circles of sticks and stones, or the imprint of his own hand dipped in mud forming a Mantra-like circle on the wall. These sculptures can be disassembled and reconstructed as necessary, which would seem to be ecologically sound.

Wolfgang Laib uses basic organic and fragile materials – milk, pollen, rice – which are for him full of symbols and possess an energy and power which he says he could not himself create. His rice houses, which are laid directly on the floor, are wooden structures covered with metal, pierced with a small, round hole and filled with rice to the point of overflowing. Laib says: 'They have the form of a house and also of a reliquary of the Middle Ages or of a Muslim tomb, which contains the bones of saints.'

a stone's throw from the Japanese Pavilion, there was a sculpture by Phillip King entitled *Shogun*, 1988, which incorporated hefty chunks of wood within an open metal framework. It encapsulates in a powerful piece the Westerner's notion of a Japanese warrior.

An artist who combines living trees with figures alternately carved from bark or cast in bronze, all sprouting from terracotta pots, is Giuseppe Penone. The effect is of unrestrained vegetation and the twisted, distorted sprites are undoubtedly Romantic. A more orderly, less earthbound landscape, seascape, or possibly even moonscape is Arnaldo Pomodoro's aluminium *Shield, Seashores, the Sceptres*, 1987-8, actually three separate groups of sculpture displayed together. The seashore is represented by oval elements which are seashells vastly enlarged and out of scale, as in a Surrealist dreamscape. The sceptres are 'the antennae of the future, the tribal masks that rise up out of a dark wood and triumphantly stand out on the horizon of the seashores of his dreams' (Giovanni Carandente). The shield is encrusted with the 'tribal' configurations which form the heads of the sceptres and is, according to the artist, a protection against nightmares.

Mystery and perhaps a certain ambiguity, whether of form or

L to R: Wolfgang Laib, *Rice Houses* (detail), rice, wood, white metal sheet, sealing wax; Arnaldo Pomodoro, *Shield, Seashores, the Sceptres*, 1987-8, aluminium

They also contain an implicit comment on the world's starving millions. In 1977 Laib made his first *Pollen Piece*. From mid-February he collects pollen from the meadows and forests surrounding his studio and stores them in small jars, keeping the types of flowers separate. He says: 'Pollen has incredible colours which you could never paint.' They are extremely beautiful, which is his avowed aim, but one cannot help having a nagging doubt about the deprived bees.

Traditionally the Japanese have been obsessed with wood as a sacred material having magical properties, as shown by the fact that the many statues of the Buddha in their temples are more often carved in wood than cast in metal. Contemporary artists have continued this tradition of wood-carving. Shigeo Toya uses wood blocks which he works with a chainsaw or hatchet to produce deep intersecting notches. The split and indented surface is then rubbed with plaster of Paris or pigments. Toya's *Range Of Mountains*, 1985, is a group of these notched and coloured wooden boulders set on a striated circular wood base which is itself a cross-section of a treetrunk. The material quality of the wood is more important than the associations which it provokes. In this context it is interesting to record that at Venice,

content, are qualities inherent in Romanticism. Richard Deacon's shapes are open to several interpretations, some of which have literary sources hinted at in their titles. *Falling on Deaf Ears*, 1984, in galvanised steel and canvas, suggests the story of Ulysses stuffing his companions' ears with wax and strapping himself to the mast in order not to be seduced by the song of the Sirens, whilst the upthrust member may be seen as the prow of the ship or as a phallus. *For Those who have Ears No 2*, 1983, as well as its manifest biblical reference, refers to Orpheus, inspired by Rilke's 'Sonnets to Orpheus'. The intricately curved laminated wood shapes can be read as an inner ear, as breasts or buttocks; or, taking the whole configuration together, as a nesting bird; or again, and most appropriately, a lyre, Orpheus' instrument and the Romantic symbol of creativity.

Mystery is also an integral part of Alison Wilding's sculpture, which resists any attempt at literal interpretation. It is concerned with femaleness, which is emphatically not to do with feminism, but rather with what it is like to be a woman. Much of her work is to do with enclosure or protection: a larger form enfolds or contains a smaller one, as in Henry Moore's *Two Forms*, 1934, in pynkado wood (Museum of Modern Art, New York), which he

Markus Lüpertz, *Shepherd*, 1986, bronze

Alison Wilding, *Hemlock III*, 1986, lime, hemlock, lead, beeswax, pigment

said could be regarded as a mother and child, the larger form rearing over and sheltering the smaller. A similar intent is evident in Wilding's *Curvaturae*, 1985, while enclosure is more complete in *Hearth*, 1986, a single hollow monolith, slit down one side and terminating in a thin arch. Yielding to the temptation to search for equivalents, it could be seen as having a formal affinity with Piero de la Francesca's *Madonna del Parto* in a tiny chapel near Arezzo in which two angels part curtains to reveal the pregnant Madonna. It can also more obviously be seen as a vagina. Wilding reveals her interest in alchemy in *Hemlock III*, 1986, made from lime, hemlock, lead, beeswax and pigment. It is an enormously evocative piece, the dish shape of the upper element containing the poisonous ingredients. The sense of evil is palpable.

The sculptures by Shirazeh Houshiary in the early 1980s were biomorphic and archetypal. They were made of straw and earth, moulded over wooden armatures. *Listen to the Tale of the Reed*, 1982, exhibited at the Serpentine Gallery in 1984, is composed of five separate elements, zoomorphic in the variety of shapes they evoked, from man to dinosaur, inspired by a Persian legend. Since then her work has become intentionally more abstract and architectural. *Echo*, 1985, is composed of flat planes and sharp

corners, yet there is in the horizontal spread and upthrust members a suggestion of a reclining figure whose head and knees rise upwards. The indentations have a kind of lilting poetry: she says 'the works are about fragmenting the whole – there are echoes, but nothing is whole.' The intention of the work is to express the immaterial in visible terms.

Luciana Fabro is a magician. He belongs to the Arte Povera group, and uses a great range of materials to effect his transformations. At ROSC 1988 he installed a line of white eggs (they had to be pure white) which represented both perfect form and the birth of the world, expressing with minimal means a breathtakingly transcendental idea. In 1986, in the exhibition *Falls the Shadow* at the Hayward Gallery, he was represented by an installation entitled *Iconography* which, although it dates from 1975, can justifiably be considered in the context of his continuing interests in the 1980s. The work consisted of a wooden table covered with an exquisite linen tablecloth, on which were laid clear glass dishes each containing water filled up to a certain-level, and a glass object. The resonances were multiple, the clearest being an equation with the Last Supper, but after the participants had left the table.

There is another category which could be classified as Romantic, although some may consider this distasteful. For I think those sculptures which are concerned with the imminent destruction of the earth are Romantic in the same way that John Martin's apocalyptic paintings of cosmic upheavals, such as *The Great Day of His Wrath* or *The Destruction of Sodom and Gomorrah*, are indisputably Romantic.

Tony Cragg, Britain's representative at the 1988 Venice Biennale, has always been socially conscious, but his vision has darkened in recent years. Since the late 1970s he has used urban detritus, such as discarded bits of plastic and wooden objects which have long since outlived their useful life, to create sculptures that express his anxiety for the future of the human race in an increasingly man-made environment. Cragg practised only briefly as a laboratory technician, but it has left an abiding legacy in the form of an obsessive interest in chemistry, this has led to his fear for our future: it was a physicist who first split the atom. One of the most impressive pieces at Venice was a tripartite sculpture called *On the Savannah*, 1988. The three huge vessels, which are based on laboratory or engineering shapes, stand in for human and animal forms, threatening by their very size and their uncompromising anonymity. Cragg sees clearly and his honesty forces him to be a prophet of doom.

Enzo Cucchi, in common with Clemente and Paladino, is concerned with Italy's legendary and mythological past. In *A Painting which Grazes the Sea*, 1983, a stormy sky and turbulent sea are the setting for a dark ship creeping across the horizon. The sticks attached to the surface must be seen as driftwood, perhaps from a sunken boat. The ship may equally well be a battle cruiser or an evocation of Dante's barque crossing the Styx. Skulls, so often present in Cucchi's work, bob about forebodingly in the sea. The ultimate despairing sculpture is *Drawings Living in the Earth's Fear*, 1983. A blasted tree trunk stands solitary amid a devastated landscape. No living being has survived, and the scorched earth looks as if it will never bloom again. Cucchi's sculpture says it all: it is the end.

It is easier to pinpoint Romanticism in literature, music or painting than in sculpture. What could be more Romantic than Keats' 'Ode to a Nightingale' with its yearning sense of loss? Or Wagner's 'Lohengrin', with the maiden falsely accused and the knight in shining armour who arrives in a boat drawn by a swan to champion her, again resulting in loss due to her unfortunate curiosity as to his identity? Romanticism is recognisable in painting: Caspar David Friedrich's cathedrals and crucifixes in mountains, not to mention skeletons in a stalactite cave, are of the very essence, confusing religion with the pathetic fallacy. The stuff of romance is evident in Dante Gabriel Rossetti's pictures of Dante and Beatrice and of the Arthurian legend. With regard to sculpture it is infinitely harder to reach a definition. Edward Onslow Ford's *St George and the Dragon*, in the Lady Lever Art Gallery, is undoubtedly Romantic, but the First World War destroyed the notion of the warrior as hero. When Michael Sandle was commissioned to make a sculpture of *St George and the Dragon*, now sited at Dorset Rise, Blackfriars, he wanted to make the dragon the winner, but this was unacceptable to the commissioners. Metaphor and allegory, with a goodly admixture of appropriation from the past, are among the ingredients of contemporary Romanticism which has abandoned windy rhetoric in favour of a poetic equivalent.

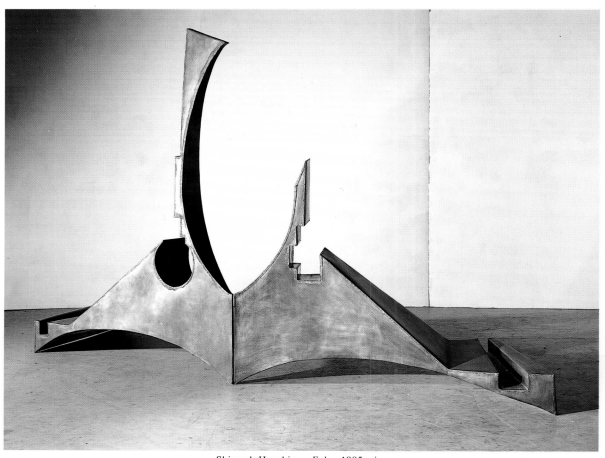

Shirazeh Houshiary, *Echo*, 1985, zinc